Walks in the

and Tillingbo

19 circular walks and 1 linear walk

described in detail

with historical places and points of interest

to engage the walker in moments of rest

along the way.

The Green Hills of Surrey

O' from Box Hill and Leith Hill the prospects are fair,
You look o'er the sweet vales of green Surrey there,
And then Surrey's dear green vales you never saw lie
Or sweeter or greener, beneath the blue sky;
O, the green hills of Surrey, the sweet hills of Surrey,
The dear hills of Surrey, I'll love till I die.

O' Dorking is pleasant and Dorking is green,
And sweet are the woods and the walks of Deepdene,
But for Dorking's sweet meadows in vain must I sigh,
And Deepdene's green woods will no more meet my eye;
But the green woods of Surrey, the sweet woods of Surrey,
The dear woods of Surrey, I'll love till I die

W C Bennett 1861

By Leslie Ham

Order this book online at www.trafford.com/07-0186
or email orders@trafford.com

Most Trafford titles are also available at major online book retailers.

© Copyright 2007 Leslie Ham.
All rights reserved. No part of this publication may be reproduced, stored in a retrieval system, or transmitted, in any form or by any means, electronic, mechanical, photocopying, recording, or otherwise, without the written prior permission of the author.

Note for Librarians: A cataloguing record for this book is available from Library and Archives Canada at www.collectionscanada.ca/amicus/index-e.html

Printed in Victoria, BC, Canada.

ISBN: 978-1-4251-1774-0

We at Trafford believe that it is the responsibility of us all, as both individuals and corporations, to make choices that are environmentally and socially sound. You, in turn, are supporting this responsible conduct each time you purchase a Trafford book, or make use of our publishing services. To find out how you are helping, please visit www.trafford.com/responsiblepublishing.html

Our mission is to efficiently provide the world's finest, most comprehensive book publishing service, enabling every author to experience success. To find out how to publish your book, your way, and have it available worldwide, visit us online at www.trafford.com/10510

 www.trafford.com

North America & international
toll-free: 1 888 232 4444 (USA & Canada)
phone: 250 383 6864 ♦ fax: 250 383 6804 ♦ email: info@trafford.com

The United Kingdom & Europe
phone: +44 (0)1865 722 113 ♦ local rate: 0845 230 9601
facsimile: +44 (0)1865 722 868 ♦ email: info.uk@trafford.com

10 9 8 7 6 5 4 3

Contents

Preface	5
Acknowledgements	6
Introduction	7
The concept	7
The style	7
The routes	7
Some Basic Information	8
Maps and navigational equipment	8
Clothing and equipment	8
Accommodation	8
Transport	8
Refreshments	8
Footpaths	8
Safety	8
Places of interest	9
GPS information	9
Maps	9
Walks routes	10
About the author	11
Walk 1 - Mickleham, Mickleham Downs, White Hill, Juniper Top, Box Hill	12
St Michaels and All Angels church, Mickleham	*13*
A flyer's memorial	*13*
Burford Bridge Hotel, Box Hill	*14*
Walk 2 - Mickleham, Box Hill, Brockham Hill, Betchworth, Brockham, River Mole	15
Peter Labelliere Headstone	*16*
Box Hill fort	*16*
St Michael's church, Betchworth	*17*
Crop fields at Betchworth looking towards Brockham Hill	*18*
Walk 3 - Stepping Stones, River Mole, Deepdene, The Glory Wood, The Nower, North Downs	19
Deepdene Woods	*20*
Staines Ramblers at The Temple, The Nower	*21*
Dorking below Box Hill	*22*
Walk 4 - Westhumble, Bookham, Ranmore Common	24
Fanny Burney plaque at Westhumble	*25*
Plaques at the former Royal School of Church Music, Westhumble	*26*
Walk 5 - Milton Heath, The Lake, Squires Farm, Coldharbour, Leith Hill, Greensand Way, The Rookery	27
Leith Hill Tower	*28*
At the Rookery	*29*
Walk 6 - Westcott, Park Farm, Abinger Roughs, Crossways Farm, Townhurst Wood, Bushy Wood, The Wilderness, The Rookery	31
Westcott village	*32*
Wilberforce Memorial, Abinger Roughs	*33*
Walk 7 - Friday Street, Wotton, North Downs, Westcott, The Rookery	35
The pond at Friday Street	*36*
Stowe Maries, Westcott	*37*
Walk 8 - Friday Street, Broadmoor, Tillingbourne spring, Coldharbour, Leith Hill Place, Site of The Old Observatory	39
Tilling Spring	*40*
Boundary stone and Azimuth pillar at The Old Observatory, Abinger	*42*
Walk 9 - Holmbury St Mary, Somerset Hill, Leith Hill, Abinger Bottom, Abinger Common	44
Village well and Goddards Abinger Common	*45*
Walk 10 - Holmbury St Mary, Winterfold Hill, Raynards Hill, Pitch Hill, Duke of Kent school, Holmbury Hill Fort Somerset Hill	47

4   The Surrey Hills

Judge James seat at Raynards Hill 49
Walk 11 - Peaslake, Brook, Blackheath forest, Roman Temple, Dick's Hill 51
   Peaslake village stores 52
   Roman Temple, Farley Heath 53
Walk 12 - Gomshall, Abinger Common, Sutton Abinger, Paddington Farm,
        Broomy Downs, Hackhurst Down, Netley Park 55
   Village Stocks Abinger Common 56
   St James church, Abinger Common 56
   The Volunteer, Sutton Abinger. 57
Walk 13 - Shere, Newlands Corner, St Martha's Hill, Albury 59
   Village well, Shere 59
   Albury Down 60
   Apostolic church, Albury 61
   Lower St, Shere 61
Walk 14 - Shere, Gomshall, Peaslake, Farley Green, Brook, Little London 62
   Gomshall Mill, Gomshall. 63
   Plaque at St James' church, Shere 63
   Outline of Anchoress's enclosure St James' church, Shere 63
   Hurtwood Inn, Peaslake. 64
   Ramblers in the Surrey Hills 65
Walk 15 - Newlands corner, Albury, Blackheath forest, Farley Green,
        Brook, Albury Estate, Silent Pool, North Downs 66
   A painter at Newlands Corner 67
   Village shop, Albury 67
   Not The Old Pharmacy, Albury. 68
   A very silent – Silent Pool – during a drought 2006 69
Walk 16 - Blackheath, Blackheath Forest, Farley Green, Albury Park, Albury ... 71
   Albury Park. 72
Walk 17 - Pewley Down, St Martha's Hill, Waterloo Pond, Blackheath,
        Wonersh Common, Chinthurst Hill, East Shalford 74
   St Martha's church, St Martha's Hill. 75
Walk 18 - Wey Navigation, Wey South path (Disused railway),
        Downs Link, St Martha's Hill, North Downs Way, Pewley Down ... 78
   Pewley Down 80
Walk 19 - Tillingbourne spring, Wotton, Abinger Hammer, Gomshall,
        Shere, Albury, Waterloo Pond, Chilworth, East Shalford,
        Wey Navigation 82
   Pond at the source of the Tillingbourne. 84
   Tillingbourne, Abinger Hammer 85
   Jack the Hammer 86
   Abinger Hammer 86
   Gomshall Mill over the Tillingbourne 87
Walk 20 - Box Hill, Brockham Hill, Deepdene, The Glory Wood, The Nower,
        Anstiebury, Leith Hill, Somerset Hill, Holmbury Hill, Pitch Hill,
        Reynards Hill, Winterfold Hill, Barnett Hill, Chinthurst Hill,
        Pewley Down, St Martha's Hill, Newlands Corner, Hackhurst
        Downs, Ranmore Common, Stepping Stones, Box Hill 90
   Staines Ramblers at Box Hill 93
   Village well and Green, Brockham 93
   Coldharbour village. 96
   All weather walkers in the Surrey Hills. 97
   Holmbury Hill 98
   Chinthurst tower 99
   St Barnabas church Ranmore 102
   Which way now guys? 103
Local History Notes. 104
   The Millennium Stone plaque in St James' churchyard, Shere 125
Village signs 126
Useful addresses and websites 127
Index 129

Preface

Walking is a basic movement of mankind. He might have walked from place to place for survival, to follow a food supply, or avoid harsh or changing weather patterns, then later to tend his captive animals and manage his crops. It is only since mankind had conquered his basic requirements and safeguarded his food supply that he chose to walk for reasons not particularly connected with survival. With walking we need only free time to become available to us as a pleasure rather than a necessity as the act of walking costs little. This has led in the past to a perceived division of attitude in the social classes – those who rode and those who walked – the wealthy and the poor.

However, there have been many notable walkers in history Poets, Intellectuals, Pilgrims, Explorers and Ramblers among them. Probably some of the first walkers to be noticed were the Pilgrims walking great distances for their faith.

England's coast offer us the opportunity to "walk the boundaries" of the meeting of land sea and air. Our hills and forests offer us sights and scenes familiar to our ancestors. Our rivers and waterways offer us tranquillity. Meadows offer up an unhurried peace denied in a modern age. Opportunities abound in whatever environment pleases.

Walking is easy providing one is fit and able, as implied by the commonly used phrase "It's a walk in the park". In reasonable health it's just a question of putting one foot in front of the other and repeating it. Walking is the art of the lingering revelation. Something spied in the distance comes to us slowly and quietly. The distant feature is upon us, then offering new horizons to the adventurous. Walking looses its measurable distances in favour of the passage of time.

Walking is one of life's natural ways to maintain the health that each of us was probably and thankfully born with. It needn't be a marathon or a daunting hill climb, a walk can be broken down into easy segments enabling those who thought they couldn't, can. With reasonable health walking is always available to those who have denied it a place in their lives.

Walking for pleasure allows us to create our own plan, when to walk, where to walk, how far to walk, at what speed, where to pause;

> What is this life if full of care
> We have no time to stand and stare

It offers us an opportunity to expand an interest be it in flora and fauna, ornithology, lepidoptera, wildlife, geography, geology, history, architecture, even literature and music, therefore walking provides us with that vehicle. It allows us to observe at a more leisurely pace lending itself to thought and ponder. It is an antidote to modern speed living where time passes by unchecked. It lends itself to personal achievement at one's own will in a governing age.

LH
Weybridge 2007

Acknowledgements

Route checkers, John Betteridge, John Bradbury, Bill Grace, Jean Reeves, Greg Moncrieff
Additional photography, John Betteridge, Eric Lucas
British Library, London
Guildford library
Weybridge library
Dorking library
Public Record Office, Kew
Kathy Atherton, Dorking Local History Group
Janet Balchin Ewhurst History Society
Various members of Surrey local history groups
Barry Pickering for proof reading

Front cover pictures
Leith Hill tower, Abinger Hatch ph, Tillingbourne at Shere, Tilling Spring Surrey hills bluebells

Rear cover pictures
Village signs in the Surrey hills

Author's Note

Every care has been taken in the preparation of this book. The walks have been independently checked and are believed to be correct at the time of publication. However, no guarantee can be given that it contains no errors or omissions and neither the author nor the publishers can accept any responsibility for loss, damage or inconvenience resulting from the use of this book.

Please remember that the countryside is continually changing: hedges and fences may be removed or re-sited: footbridges and river banks may suffer flood damage: footpaths may be re-routed or ploughed over and not re-instated (as the law requires): concessionary paths may be closed. If you do encounter any such problems please let the publishers know, and please report any obstructions to rights of way to the relevant local authority.

Introduction

The concept
This book of local walks to the Surrey Hills follows on two long distance historical walking guidebooks which I wrote both taking 3 years each to put to bed. Into those two books went six continuous years of planning, researching of routes and relevant information, walking the routes, researching and writing up the history and then writing up the book, it was far from finished at that point. Then followed the route checking by excellent and helpful volunteers from the Rambler's Association together with great help and enthusiasm from historical groups who kindly and willingly checked the historical contents, all without whom I could not have published successfully.

After lots of thought I decided to take a sabbatical from the writing of long distance guidebooks and concentrate on the somewhat shorter project of compiling a book of walks local to myself in the wonderfully delightful Surrey Hills, one of my first loves in my 45 years of walking. The green hills and valleys, picturesque villages and hamlets, forests and brooks of the country idyll in which I empathize with Bennett above. I felt that this had to be documented, as others had done before, but now in my own hand.

I have therefore compiled a book of walks centred on what I would consider to be the most evocative parts of the Surrey Hills. I hope that walkers of all ages will find tranquillity, together with sights and sounds pleasing to the senses.

The style
I have decided to construct the walks that would encourage the non-walker to participate alongside the seasoned and committed walker. Some walks are of an easy nature, others with a little effort expended to gain a hill top offering fine views and bracing air but all the more rewarding.

The Routes
The walks are based from locations in such a way as they lend themselves for two walks to be combined for those who prefer greater distances. It is also possible to walk sections of routes to form a linear walk. I have constructed the walks that allow the walker to switch between walks to enable a variation of route devised by the reader who may wish to mix and match from the routes described. The longer walks can be walked in sections.

Some basic information

Maps and navigation equipment

I would hope that every walker novice or experienced can find their way with the aid of this book but having said that it is always useful to have the appropriate map and a compass with you. I have given some Ordnance Survey grid references at key points to help those who like additionally to use their GPS navigational equipment. The maps in this book, will, I hope, also be of great use in planning your days walking. Each walk has its own map. I have decided not to include a map showing all the routes together as the scale would be too small to be of great use and hope that the more detailed individual maps will suffice.

Clothing and equipment

It would be advisable to have a good pair of walking boots or shoes but all these walks can be done in good trainers. In wet weather some paths may be muddy.

Accommodation

Should the walker need accommodation I have listed the nearest Tourist Information Centres where this information can be obtained.

Transport

It is possible to complete most of these walks by using public transport but in some areas buses may be infrequent and many do not operate on Sundays. Please check the information regarding buses at the back of this book. It is possible to join most of these routes by public transport at various points along them, it is therefore not vital to join the route at the start point given. Please obtain copies of the Bus and Train guide No's 7 and 8 from main bus stations. There are car parks or areas to park at or near the start/finish locations.

Refreshments

Cafes, tea shops and public houses are mentioned but I would always advise walkers to carry their own supplies of water, particularly on hot days.

Footpaths

All the footpaths in this guide are official paths as shown on the appropriate Ordnance Survey maps. They are all well used by locals, ramblers and visitors alike. There are no problems with access on the walks described.

> NB. In Albury Park it is permitted to walk along the access road from New Rd although this is not marked as a footpath on the OS map.

Safety

On occasions walks may cross busy roads or active railway lines where great care should be taken. It is always best to walk along lanes or roads where you can best be seen by motorists in both directions.

Places of Interest

I have given more detailed information regarding the many places of interest along the walks to enliven moments of rest. Additionally they are numbered in the walk description with a detailed explanation at the back of the book.

GPS information

For the benefit of those walkers interested in gadgets I have included OS GB grid references at many locations to enable the route to be planned, or get lost more accurately. It might also prove useful should anyone wish to walk the routes in the reverse direction.

Maps

The maps in this book are presented conventionally (North at the top). Arrows denote the described direction of the walk. They are intended to give a general idea of the route of the walk. I have chosen not to include the historical locations on the maps in order to keep them uncluttered. Although you will be able to find your way following the route descriptions I would always recommend that walkers carry the appropriate Ordnance Survey map noted at the top of each walk.

N.B. Please do not be put off by the frequent use of Ordnance Survey grid references in this book, in the main they are there as extra information and for those walkers who wish to make use of them. The walks can be walked without knowledge of grid references.

>The cuckoo she's a merry bird, she sings as she flies;
>She brings us good tidings and tells us no lies
>She sucks all small birds' eggs to make her voice clear
>And never sings "Cuckoo" till summer draws near.

Walk Routes

1. 13kms 8 miles — Mickleham, Mickleham Downs, White Hill, Juniper Top, Box Hill.
2. 14 kms 8¾ miles — Mickleham, Box Hill, Brockham Hill, Betchworth, Brockham, River Mole.
3. 14.5kms 9 miles — Stepping Stones, River Mole, Deepdene, The Glory Wood, The Nower, North Downs.
4. 12 kms 7½ miles — Westhumble, Bookham, Ranmore Common.
5. 16 kms 10 miles — Milton Heath, The Lake, Squires Farm, Coldharbour, Leith Hill, Greensand Way, The Rookery.
6. 14kms 8¾ miles — Westcott, Park Farm, Abinger Roughs, Crossways Farm, Townhurst Wood, Bushy Wood, The Wilderness, The Rookery.
7. 13kms 8 miles — Friday Street, Wotton, North Downs, Westcott, The Rookery.
8. 14kms 8¾ miles — Friday Street, Broadmoor, Tillingbourne spring, Coldharbour, Leith Hill Place, Site of The Old Observatory.
9. 13kms 8 miles — Holmbury St Mary, Somerset Hill, Leith Hill, Abinger Bottom, Abinger Common.
10. 15.8kms 10 miles — Holmbury St Mary, Winterfold Hill, Raynards Hill, Pitch Hill, Duke of Kent school, Holmbury Hill Fort, Somerset Hill.
11. 12.5kms 7¾ miles — Peaslake, Brook, Blackheath forest, Roman Temple, Dick's Hill.
12. 14kms 8¾ miles — Gomshall, Abinger Common, Sutton Abinger, Paddington Farm, Broomy Downs, Hackhurst Down, Netley Park.
13. 12.2kms 7¾ miles — Shere, Newlands Corner, St Martha's Hill, Albury.
14. 13kms 8 miles — Shere, Gomshall, Peaslake, Farley Green, Brook, Little London.
15. 13.5kms 8½ miles — Newlands Corner, Albury, Blackheath forest, Farley Green, Brook, Albury Estate, Silent Pool, North Downs.
16. 12kms 7½ miles — Blackheath, Blackheath Forest, Farley Green, Albury Park, Albury.
17. 16kms 10 miles — Pewley Down, St Martha's Hill, Waterloo Pond, Blackheath, Wonersh Common, Chinthurst Hill, East Shalford.
18. 14.5kms 9 miles — Wey Navigation, Wey South path (Disused railway), Downs Link, St Martha's Hill, North Downs Way, Pewley Down.
19. 22.5kms 14 miles — Tillingbourne spring, Wotton, Abinger Hammer, Gomshall, Shere, Albury, Waterloo Pond, Chilworth, East Shalford, Wey Navigation.
20. 69.2kms 44 miles — Box Hill, Brockham Hill, Deepdene, The Glory Wood, The Nower, Anstiebury, Leith Hill, Somerset Hill, Holmbury Hill, Pitch Hill, Reynards Hill, Winterfold Hill, Barnett Hill, Chinthurst Hill, Pewley Down, St Martha's Hill, Newlands Corner, Hackhurst Downs, Ranmore Common, Stepping Stones, Box Hill.

About the Author

Leslie Ham is the author of *The Orange Way*, a 350 mile long distance path following the route of the march of Prince William of Orange from Brixham to London in 1688. He is also the author of *The Nelson Way* a 424 mile walk from Burnham Thorpe in Norfolk to HMS Victory in Portsmouth. Leslie's interest in walking began in the 1960's in the North Downs, later completing many of the Long Distance footpaths in Southern England. These included the South Downs Way, North Downs Way, Thames Path, Ridgeway, Vanguard Way, Greensand Way, Thames Valley Heritage Walk, London Countryside Way and several canal side routes. Abroad he has trekked on five Continents, including the Himalayas, New Zealand, China, South Africa, mainland France, Corsica, Spain, Romania, Patagonia, Peru, Bolivia, Chile and Mali.

In addition to walking his other main interests include travel, photography, history, genealogy, archaeology, music, poetry, modern art, target shooting, computers and things art deco.

Photo E Lucas

A resident of Weybridge for 35 years, Leslie was born in Burnley, Lancashire. He spent his formative years in Blackpool but has also lived in Kirkham, Hucknall, Nottingham, Derby, Blackburn and several locations in West London. From 1957 he spent two years doing his National Service in Aldershot, Cyprus and Jordan. In 1960 he joined BOAC, which later merged with BEA to become British Airways and spent a total of 35 interesting years at London Airport.

Since he took early retirement in 1995 he has thoroughly enjoyed his freedom and concentrated on the above with difficulty. After completing *The Orange Way* and *The Nelson Way* he then looked around for an idea for a third book. He finally decided to take a sabbatical from long distance walks to concentrate on walks local to him in the Surrey Hills where he first began his interest in walking.

Walk 1
Mickleham, Mickleham Downs, White Hill, Juniper Top and Box Hill

Map:	OS Explorer 146
Start/Finish points:	The car park by Ryka's Cafe below Box Hill on the A24 road at TQ1719 5202
Distance:	13kms (8 miles)
Time:	3hrs
Transport:	Rail: Box Hill and Westhumble, Dorking, Deepdene
	Bus: Westhumble, Dorking, Deepdene, Box Hill
Places of interest:	Flint cottage, Stane St, Cherkley Court, White Hill, Juniper Top, Juniper Hall, Box Hill, Box Hill fort, River Mole Stepping Stones, Burford Bridge Hotel.
Refreshments: café	Ryka's cafe at the car park, National Trust Box Hill, Burford Bridge Hotel, *Stepping Stones ph* Westhumble.
Local History Notes:	10, 13, 22, 35, 36, 46
Walk description:	A circular walk in a hilly historical area. In two places there are some steps to negotiate. Magnificent hilltop views of the Weald and the South Downs and particularly overlooking the town of Dorking.

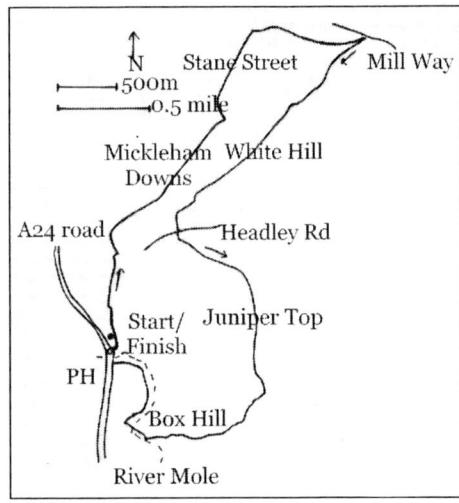

The route

Exit the car park by Ryka's Cafe *(at TQ1719 5202)* at the rear and cross over the road *(Old London Rd)* towards Box Hill. Go through a gap in the fence and turn left up a track. Soon at a Y-junction bear left and

Walk 1

keep parallel to the road *(Old London Rd)*. Exit in the left-hand corner at Zig Zag Rd. *(Flint cottage is 100m along Zig Zag Rd.)* Cross over Old London Rd and turn right then continue on the left-hand side of the road *(signed Mickleham)*. Later ascend steps to a higher level footpath. Soon pass a gated entrance to Fredley Manor. In a further 150m bear right up steps to gain the road level at a bus stop at TQ1719 5275 diagonally opposite the entrance to Juniper Hall

Cross over the road walk up Headley Lane opposite. In 25m turn left and go forward and take the left of two broad tracks leading uphill. After 850m at a cross track go forward into Box Hill Estate.

Optional detour: At this cross track you may detour left for 600m to Mickleham village and St Michael and All Angels church. Return the same way.

St Michael and All Angels Church, Mickleham

A flyer's memorial
St Michael and all Angels churchyard

Photo's L Ham

Keep ahead on the main track ignoring others. After 800m at a T-junction of tracks at TQ1808 5385 turn left uphill. At the top of the rise the path bears right, which then becomes Stane St. In 700m at a cross track at TQ1837 5467 turn right *(signed Mill Way 2/3 of a mile)*. On reaching a lane *(Mill Way)* at TQ1934 5458 turn very sharp right and walk on bearing about 240 degrees.

After 900m reach a clearing at Mickleham Downs. Follow the path veering round to the left and walk on a broad green track on the top of White Hill. Keeping to the left of this broad green track bear left into a wooded area at TQ1797 5343. At a junction of tracks turn left slightly downhill soon turning right. At a clearing at TQ1781 5317, by a seat on the right, continue on ahead. The path bears left and goes steeply downhill and then down some steps to gain a road *(Headley Rd)* opposite Whitehill car park at TQ1770 5293.

Cross over the road and walk through the car park. Exit at the back of the car park on a broad track. In a few metres at a Y-junction bear left through the kissing gate to the left of a gate and continue on the left-hand track ahead up Juniper Top. Continue on up the hill on a broad grassy track. At the top of the hill keep to the right-hand side and go through a kissing gate at TQ1835 5242 next to a gate and continue on the broad track ahead. After 750m at a Y-junction take the right-hand fork and in a few more metres at a cross track continue on ahead. At a five track junction at TQ1825 5154 maintain direction. The path eventually emerges to an open space bear left before it and gain a road through a car park.

Cross over the road and turn right and take a footpath alongside the road, which bears left down to the viewing point on Box Hill at TQ1797 5118.

Re-gain the road and continue on walking through the National Trust area and to a track leading left behind a small car park. In a few metres reach Box Hill fort. Here turn about and walk back through the National Trust area turning right on a track to reach a cross track before Swiss Cottage. Here turn right and at a junction of tracks turn left. Follow the path round and just before an open area turn sharp right at TQ1777 5119 down shallow steps. Continue down more steps to the bottom of Box Hill.

Here go forward on the broad track to reach the River Mole stepping stones. Cross over the stepping stones and turn right and walk to the footbridge. *(If the River mole is in flood you can turn right at the stepping stones and walk to the footbridge and cross over it and then turn right through the kissing gate.)* Turn left through a kissing gate before the footbridge and enter a field with the River Mole on the right. Walk on the grassy track alongside the river which slowly bears left. Exit the field through a kissing gate by Burford Bridge and gain the A24 road.

Burford Bridge Hotel, Box Hill   Photo J Betteridge

Here turn right and cross the bridge. Soon at a roundabout bear right along Old London Rd and walk past the Burford Bridge Hotel. In a few metres cross over the road and turn left into the car park by Ryka's Cafe.

Walk 2
Mickleham, Box Hill, Brockham Hill, Betchworth, Brockham and the River Mole

Map:	OS Explorer 146
Start/Finish points:	The car park by Ryka's Cafe below Box Hill on the A24 road at TQ1719 5202
Distance:	14kms (8¾ miles)
Time:	3¼ hrs
Transport:	Rail: Box Hill and Westhumble, Dorking, Deepdene
	Bus: Box Hill, Betchworth, Brockham
Places of interest:	Burford Bridge Hotel, Labelliere headstone, Box Hill, Box Hill fort, Betchworth, Brockham, Stepping Stones, River Mole.
Refreshments:	Ryka's cafe at the car park, Burford Bridge Hotel, *Dolphin Inn ph*, Betchworth, *Duke's Head or Royal Oak ph's* and shops Brockham village, *Stepping Stones ph* Westhumble
Local History Notes:	8, 10, 12, 13, 46
Walk description:	Hills, views, villages, rivers.

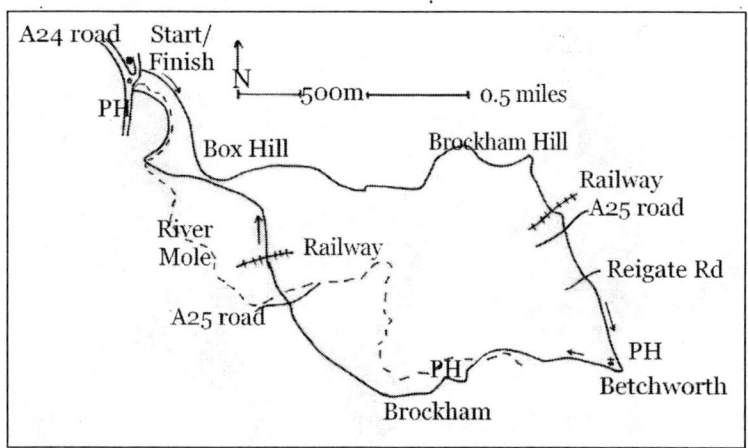

The route

Exit the car park by Ryka's Cafe at TQ1719 5202 and cross over the road *(Old London Rd)* towards Box Hill. Go through a gap in the fence and turn right and walk up a steep stepped track to ascend the side of Box Hill. The steps give way to a steep chalky track. Keep to the left of a tree line and walk round its left-hand edge and carry on up the hill. Later bear right to follow a broad chalk track ignoring others. Where the track narrows go forward to pass a stone headstone, the inscription reads *(Major Peter Labelliere aged 75 an eccentric resident of Dorking was buried here head downwards 11th July 1800)*.

The Surrey Hills

Peter Labelliere Headstone   Photo L Ham

Continue on and in 80m where the path begins to go downhill at a T-junction, turn left by a centrally located tree trunk. Carry on and soon reach Swiss Cottage on the right, a plaque reads *(John Logie Baird 1888-1946 the inventor of television lived here Swiss Cottage 1929-1932)*. Here bear left and left again and walk on past the National Trust shop area. Beyond a small car park turn left down a broad track. In a few metres reach Box Hill fort.

Box Hill fort   Photo L Ham

Here do an about turn and walk back past the NT shop area and continue alongside the road. The path then veers away from the road and goes down to an observation and trig point on Box Hill at TQ1797 5118.

Walk left *(east)* away from the observation point along the North Downs Way. After 100m at a Y-junction bear left. Maintain this path ignoring others. Go through a gate and later go through a second gate and carry on ahead. Maintain direction, at a Y-junction bear right ignoring other tracks. In a wooded area the path dips down and up steps twice before continuing slowly downhill through the woodland. Later the path swings sharp left up steps. At the top of the steps turn right. At an inverse Y-junction go forward down steps.

Walk 2   17

At the bottom of the steps at a T-junction of tracks turn left. At a Y-junction at TQ1956 5133, by a notice board, bear right. Just before some steps, look to the left, and notice the grave of "Quick" *(An English Thoroughbred 1936-1944)*. Carry on down the steps to a T-junction of tracks, here turn right downhill. Continue on downhill to reach a T-junction of tracks by a notice board, here turn right leaving the North Down Way.

The track later goes left *(hard to spot)* and then over a cross track *(Pilgrims' Way)*. Continue forward and go over a step stile and enter a field. Carry on ahead across the field on a faint track on bearing about 140 degrees. Cross over a bridge over the railway and go over a step stile and enter another field. Walk half left for 50m then turn right to walk along the left-hand side of a tree line. Cross over a step stile and reach the A25 road.

St Michael's church, Betchworth
Photo L Ham

Cross this very busy road and go over a step stile and enter a small field. Cross the field slightly left on a faint track. Exit in the left-hand corner of the field over step stile and continue on ahead alongside a fence on the right. Follow the path which later goes left and becomes enclosed. Later walk behind residences and halfway along take an enclosed path between residences which emerge at a road by a post office.

Cross over the road and turn left and in 30m turn right by a bus stop on a surfaced path. Eventually the path meets a road, continue on along it in the same direction. At a T-junction *(on the left)* by the *Dolphin Inn*, Betchworth, turn right up a surfaced track on the Greensand Way.

Enter the churchyard through an arched doorway of St Michael's church Betchworth. Walk on through the churchyard exiting through a gate. Cross over an access lane and continue on the track ahead. Go through a gate and enter a large field, continue on its left-hand edge *(later note the WWII pillbox on the left)*. Exit through a gate and carry on ahead. Cross a footbridge over a ditch. At a T-junction with a broad track turn left ignoring the path on the right. At a Y-junction go left over a footbridge over the River Mole and continue on a narrow surfaced track. Cross over a bridge and go through a gate at the terminal point of an access lane in Brockham.

Here turn right and walk on past the *Dukes Head* and the *Royal Oak* public houses and bear left across the village Green. Cross over the road passing by the village well and go down Olds School Lane. Just after a bridge and where the lane goes left, bear right up a broad unsurfaced track. In 400m where the Greensand Way goes left, continue on ahead. Walk in between the two parts of Betchworth Park Golf Course. Eventually the path merges with the access drive to the golf course club house. Walk down the access drive and turn right to reach the A25 road.

Cross over this very busy road and go down the access road opposite and pass the entrance to Wyevale Garden Centre. At the end of the road go over a footbridge over the River Mole and continue on the disused lane ahead. Meet a lane *(Box hill Rd)* on a bend.

Continue on in the same direction and walk underneath a railway bridge. In a further 375m at TQ1823 5088 bear left on a broad track. At a Y-junction take the left fork and in 40m go over a step stile by a gate and take the immediate left fork. Maintain this track ignoring others. Later go through a kissing gate then the track begins to descend. At a T-junction of tracks turn left downhill and continue down the steps to the bottom of the hill.

Crop fields at Betchworth looking towards Brockham Hill   Photo L Ham

At the bottom of the hill go forward on the broad track to the River Mole stepping stones, or, turn right and soon cross over the footbridge. *(At the stepping stones you can still turn right and walk to the footbridge.)* Having crossed over the stepping stones turn right alongside the river and walk up to the footbridge. *(If you used the footbridge you are already at that position).* Go through the kissing gate and into a field, with the River Mole on the right. Walk on the grassy track alongside the river which slowly bears left. Exit through a kissing gate by Burford Bridge and go up to the A24 road.

Here turn right and cross the bridge. Soon at a roundabout bear right along Old London Rd and walk past the Burford Bridge Hotel. Cross over the road into the car park by Ryka's Cafe.

Walk 3
Stepping Stones, River Mole, Deepdene, The Glory Wood, The Nower, North Downs

Map:	OS Explorer 146
Start/Finish points:	Stepping Stones car park on the A24 at TQ1710 5135 south of Burford Bridge
Distance:	14.5kms (9 miles)
Time:	3½ hrs
Transport:	Rail: Box Hill and Westhumble, Dorking, Deepdene
	Bus: Westhumble, Dorking, Deepdene, Box Hill
Places of interest:	River Mole Stepping Stones, Burford Bridge Hotel, Deepdene, The Temple, Denbies Vineyard, Burford corner
Refreshments:	Burford Bridge Hotel Mickleham, Queens Head ph Horsham Rd Dorking, *Stepping Stones ph* Westhumble, Denbies Wine Estate
Local History Notes:	10, 20, 21, 22, 43, 46, 56
Walk description:	A circular hilly walk overlooking the town of Dorking from its surrounding hills offering fine views.

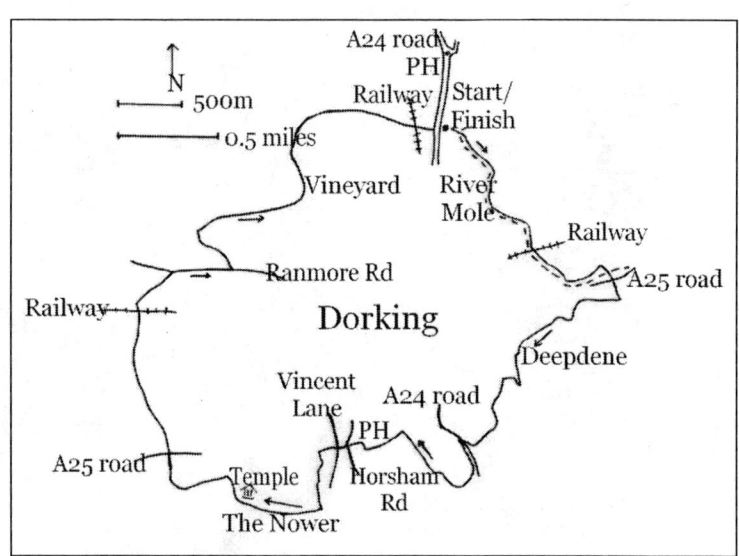

The route

Exit the rear of the Stepping Stones car park on the right-hand broad track leading to the stepping stones over the River Mole.

> *(Should you not wish to cross the stepping stones you may walk along the path to the left and cross over a footbridge lower down the river and continue on the path to meet up with this path at a junction on the other side.)*

Having crossed the stepping stones or the footbridge over the River Mole continue on the track leading up Box Hill. At the point of the second flight of steps at TQ1742 5115 bear right on a signed track *(NT Riverside Walk)*. Follow this path through the trees and back down to the riverside. Go through a kissing gate and walk alongside the River Mole on the right-hand edge of a field soon passing by wartime defenses. Later the path becomes well-defined. On approaching an arched railway bridge go through a gate and continue on underneath the bridge. Exit through a gate and continue on alongside the river. At a footbridge over the river *(do not cross)* continue on ahead. Exit through a kissing gate and continue on the broad track ahead. At a T-junction with a disused lane turn right and immediately cross over a footbridge *(Boxhill Bridge)* over the River Mole. Join the terminal point of an access road now to Wyedale Garden Centre. Continue on ahead to the A25 road.

Cross over this busy road and go forward up the access road to Betchworth Park Golf Club. At a T-junction of roads turn left uphill. At the top of the hill where the road swings right into the car park turn right on a footpath. Beyond the car park ignore a path on the left and soon at a Y-junction of tracks take the right fork. At a point about 600m along the track, and, below your feet is a railway tunnel. Maintain this track to a point where it joins a narrow surfaced lane, continue on ahead in the same direction soon reaching a road.

There was a young lady from Dorking
Who bought a large bonnet for walking
But its colour and size
So bedazzled her eyes
That she very soon went back to Dorking

Edward Lear 1846

Here turn left and in about 200m turn sharp right on a road *(Deepdene Wood)* here joining the Greensand Way. At the first T-junction on the left *(signed to No's 5-29)*, turn left. Almost at the end of the road *(Deepdene End)* turn right on a grassy track. Where the track begins to descend, at a Y-junction, take the right fork down hard to spot steps leading downhill through rhododendron bushes. At the bottom of the hill at a cross track turn right. Continue on down to the A24 road.

Deepdene Woods
Photo L Ham

Cross over this very busy road and turn left. Pass the end of Chart Lane and in a few metres bear right into The Glory Wood. At a Y-junction take the right

Walk 3

fork. At a T-junction turn right. At a junction of tracks bear right and go through a gate. Exit the wood to an open area and in 20m at a Y-junction, before a seat, bear right downhill.

Exit The Glory Wood proper through a gate and continue on the unsurfaced access road ahead. At a T-junction turn left and where it meets another road on a bend continue on ahead in the same direction. In about 150m turn right along Peacock Walk. In just over 100m turn left on a narrower enclosed surfaced footpath. Exit the path by the *Queen's Head* public house on Horsham Rd. Dorking.

Cross over Horsham Rd and turn right for a few metres to the junction. Turn left along South St and walk up to a T-junction with Falkland Rd/Vincent Lane.

Cross over the end of Falkland Rd and turn right and in a few metres turn left up a surfaced enclosed path. At the top meet the terminal point of a road *(Nower Rd)* here continue on ahead. At a road junction *(West Bank)* turn left and walk to the end to reach a T-junction.

Staines Ramblers at The Temple, The Nower Photo L Ham

Here turn right and in 20m cross over the road and bear left past a wide gate. Go forward alongside a tall hedgerow to its corner point before a large open grassy area, here turn left. At the end of the tree line at a junction of tracks by a left entrance gate continue on the uphill track. At the top at a Y-junction of tracks bear right and walk over The Nower. Maintain this track with glimpses of views to left and right for 700m to reach The Temple. Continue on past The Temple soon passing a wooden barrier and go forward down a steep track. At the bottom of the hill at a junction of tracks bear left, soon reaching a surfaced access drive here turn left.

Where the drive swings left before a residence bear right down a broad track and in 30m bear right again on an enclosed track to the right of a gate. Exit the path down steps to reach an access lane, here turn right along Milton St *(signed Link to North Downs Way)*. Exit Milton St at Old Bury Hill Stables at a T-junction with the A25.

Cross over this very busy road and go forward on the broad track opposite *(Lince Lane)*. Where the track enters a residence walk to the right of its access gate. Cross over a footbridge with a step stile and enter a field. Cross the field on bearing about 320 degrees aiming for a step stile in a hedgerow. Exit the field over the step stile and enter a larger crop field and go forward in the same direction. Cross over a cross track and continue on ahead. Across the field enter a wooded area *(Clay Copse)* and continue on ahead. Exit the wood over a step stile to join a broad track, here turn left. Cross over an active railway line *(Dorking-Guildford line)* and continue on the uphill track ahead. Cross diagonally right over the Pilgrims' Way track and continue on the uphill track. Exit the track to reach Ranmore Rd at TQ1495 5025.

Dorking below Box Hill   Photo L Ham

Here turn right and in about 150m look for, and walk on, a path on the right parallel to the road. In a further 325m by a gate regain the road at TQ1541 5022.

Cross over the road diagonally left and continue up the track opposite. In 50m at a Y-junction take the right fork leading uphill. *(To the right is Denbies Wine Estate.)* At the top of the hill at a junction of tracks reach the North Downs Way at TQ1514 5061, here turn right. Go through a tall metal gate and enter Denbies Wine Estate. Carry on ahead and go through a second tall metal gate and continue on ahead. At a cross track maintain the North Downs Way ahead.

(Note: Should you wish to visit Denbies Wine Estate turn right at this junction and follow the path down to the shop and refreshment rooms.)

Soon the track becomes surfaced. Where the surfaced track swings sharp right continue on ahead on an unsurfaced track. In 30m at a cross track continue on ahead maintaining the North Downs Way downhill. Ignoring all other tracks eventually exit through a gate by a residence. Go forward underneath a railway arch *(Dorking-London line)* and walk up to the A24 road exiting through ornate gates.

Cross over the busy road, (or take the underpass 400m left,) and turn left and in 25m turn right to arrive at the Stepping Stones car park.

Walk 4
Westhumble, Bookham, Ranmore Common

Map:	OS Explorer 146
Start/Finish points:	Box Hill and Westhumble railway station or Ryka's Cafe below Box Hill on the A24 at TQ1708 5207, or Stepping Stones car park on the A24 south of Burford Bridge at TQ1710 5135.
Distance:	12kms (7½ miles) (from the railway station)
Time:	3hrs
Transport:	Rail: Box Hill and Westhumble, Dorking Bus: Westhumble, Dorking
Places of interest:	Burford Corner, Ruins of Westhumble Chapel, Polesden Lacey, St Barnabas church Ranmore
Refreshments:	*Stepping Stones ph* Westhumble, Ryka's Cafe in the car park on the A24
Local History Notes:	13, 42, 43, 56
Walk description:	Hills, woods and open spaces.

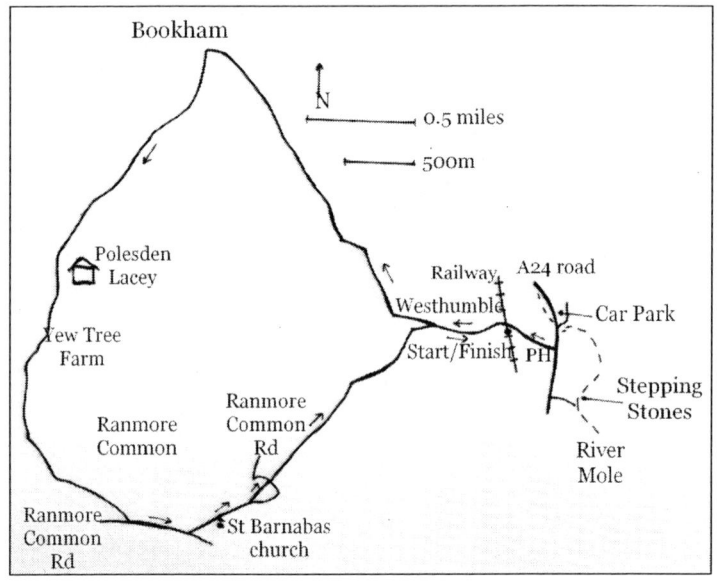

The route

From the car park by Ryka's Cafe

Exit the car park and continue along the A24 southbound crossing the end of Old London Rd. At a subway underneath the A24 walk through it and turn left. Turn right into Westhumble St. Pass by the Stepping Stones public house and then The Royal School of Church Music *(since demolished)* to reach Box Hill and Westhumble railway station.

Walk 4

From the Stepping Stones car park

Exit the car park to the A24. Turn right and walk along the A24 for 400m to the subway. Go through the subway and turn left. Turn right into Westhumble St. Pass by the *Stepping Stones* public house and then The Royal School of Church Music *(since demolished)* to reach Box Hill and Westhumble railway station.

From Box Hill and Westhumble railway station

Exit the station car park and turn left along Chapel Lane passing the entrance to Leladenes where Fanny Burney had her cottage *(Camilla)*. After 650m pass by Westhumble chapel on the left-hand side. Continue along Chapel Lane for a further 150m and turn right through a gate and enter a field. Continue uphill on the right-hand side of the field. Exit the field in the top right-hand corner through a stile by a gate and continue on the narrow track ahead into a wooded area. Exit the wooded area over a step stile to enter a field. Continue on ahead up the field in the same direction. Exit the field over a step stile to reach a lane at TQ1565 5246.

Here turn left and in just over 200m at Crabtree cottages, turn right on a broad track *(signed Bookham)*. In about 1km at a Y-junction of broad tracks take the left fork. Maintain this track ignoring others. At a multi track junction underneath power cables continue on in the same direction exiting Norbury Park. In 200m at a junction of tracks at TQ1446 5388 turn left on a broad track on bearing about 190 degrees.

Exit the track to a road at a T-junction of roads. Cross over the road and continue in the same direction on the broad track opposite alongside the road *(road signed to Polesden Lacey)*. Where the access road into Polesden Lacey goes left continue on ahead in the same direction on an unsurfaced broad track. Just past a small car park, on the left, go forward and ignore a right turn and in a few more metres take the left fork *(signed Hope Farm House etc)* at TQ1356 5273. Continue on past a residence on a surfaced access lane.

Fanny Burney plaque at Westhumble Photo L Ham

Pass under two small wooden bridges and where the lane turns sharp left continue ahead on a broad downhill track. At a T-junction of tracks turn right. At Yew Tree Farm follow the broad track round to the left. In 150m ignore the track on the right and keep to the main broad track. In a further 500m at TQ 1313 5109 and 40m before a bar-gate, turn left through a fence line and walk on through a wooded area. At a T-junction with a broad track turn right and immediately pass by a bar-gate to go forward on a grassy track in an open area. Exit from the open area through a gap in a fence line and immediately turn left on a broad track.

The track later drops down into a valley to meet a broad cross track at TQ1337 5071. Continue on ahead uphill passing through a fence line. Cross over a cross track and continue on ahead. The track eventually emerges to a road *(Ranmore Common Rd)* at Fox cottages at TQ1390 5046.

Here turn left alongside the road along the wide grass verge. 200m past the National Trust car park *(on the right)* turn left on a road, still on Ranmore Common Rd, *(signed to the Parish Church)*. 300m beyond St Barnabas church, at TQ1478 5060, turn left on a track. Emerge at a road still Ranmore Common Rd. Cross over the road and continue on the track opposite. After 450m cross over a cross track and continue on ahead.

In a further 350m meet reach a diagonal cross track at TQ1548 5134. Continue forward for a further 20m to a Y-junction where bear left. Maintain this track which goes downhill, cross over a cross track and continue on down on an enclosed track. Ignore a cross track at a stile and go forward to the end of the track which emerges at a lane at TQ1587 5163, here turn left.

After 300m turn right through a gate and continue on an enclosed track. The track exits to a lane *(Chapel Lane)*, here turn right. Continue along Chapel Lane and go over a railway bridge to arrive at Boxhill and Westhumble railway station.

Plaques at the former The Royal School of Church Music, Westhumble
Photos L Ham

To return to the car park by Ryka's Cafe continue along Chapel Lane and take the footpath on the left of the road. Pass the Royal School of Church Music *(since demolished)* and the *Stepping Stones* public house and proceed up to a T-junction with the A24. Here turn left and walk through the subway to the other side of the A24. Turn left and walk along the A24. Cross over the end of Old London Rd and walk a little further along the A24 to reach the car park by Ryka's Cafe.

To return to the Stepping Stones car park continue as above but on exiting the subway on the A24 road turn right a long the A24 road for 400m, the car park is on the left.

Walk 5
Milton Heath, The Lake, Squires Farm, Coldharbour, Leith Hill, Greensand Way, The Rookery

Map:	OS Explorer 146
Start/Finish points:	Milton Heath car park off the A25 west of Dorking, at TQ1548 4878
Distance:	16kms (10 miles)
Time:	4 hrs
Transport:	Rail: Dorking (off route) then bus to Milton Court
	Bus: Dorking to Milton Court or Guildford to Milton Court
Places of interest:	Milton Court, Anstiebury fort Coldharbour, Leith Hill, Tillingbourne, Waterfall, The Rookery.
Refreshments:	*Plough Inn ph*, Coldharbour, Leith Hill Tower (Restricted opening)
Local History Notes:	19, 32, 34, 37, 45, 55
Walk description:	Gentle climb and descent to Leith Hill, woods, hills, views and valleys.

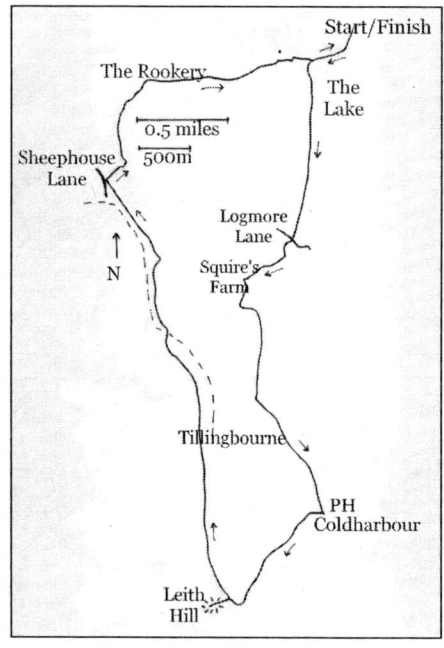

The route

Leaving Milton Heath car park at TQ1548 4878 walk along a path to the right of the notice board on bearing about 160 degrees and in 10m at a broad track continue on ahead. Keep to the right-hand track going uphill veering round to reach a lane on the Greensand Way, here turn left.

Just before a residence on a bend where the lane goes left, bear right down an access track, and in 10m where the Greensand Way goes off to the right take the left fork soon going underneath a wooden footbridge. The track emerges at an access lane at TQ1499 4840 here turn left.

At the terminal point of the lane past residences go through a metal kissing gate by a gate and continue on the track ahead. Ignore the footbridge and the bridge on the right and go forward over a lane/track and continue on the track ahead. Cross over a broad track and continue on ahead. Where a path comes in from the left by a gate, continue on over a fence stile and enter a field. Walk along the right-hand edge. Exit in the top right-hand corner of the field over a step stile to go forward on a track between tree lines. Go over a log bridge that supports a step stile over a ditch and enter a field. Continue up the left-hand edge. Exit the field almost in the left-hand corner over a step stile by a gate to gain a lane.

Cross over the lane and continue on the track opposite *(signed Squire's Farm)*. At the farm walk between the farm buildings and farmhouse and continue on a track that goes round to the left beyond the farm buildings. Then enter a wooded area. After about 300m at a Y-junction at TQ1429 4613 take the left fork. At a broad cross track on a bend at TQ1447 4556 cross over the track and continue on the track opposite going uphill. At a T-junction by a residence at TQ1445 4521 turn left. This broad track is known as Wolvens Lane. At a 5 track junction at TQ1488 4469 continue on in the same direction on bearing about 140 degrees. Maintain this broad track ignoring all others eventually emerging to a surfaced lane in Coldharbour. At a T-junction at TQ1511 4410 reach the village of Coldharbour opposite *The Plough Inn* the highest public house in South East England.

Leith Hill Tower
Photo L Ham

Optional detour to Anstiebury Hill fort: Facing The Plough public house in Coldharbour walk left along the lane. After about 300m at a lane junction turn right and in about 100m reach an entrance to the fort on the right. Return to Coldharbour village the same way.

Here turn right and walk past a telephone box on the left and continue on a broad track alongside a row of residences on the left. At a Y-junction take the right fork *(signed to the Tower and cricket field)*. Later pass Coldharbour cricket pitch on the right, the highest cricket pitch in South East England. After the cricket pitch, at a Y-junction, take the left fork. Maintain this broad obvious track ignoring others. When the track starts to go downhill meet a four track junction. Here turn right and in 10m take the right-hand fork downhill. The track descends to another multi track junction where it meets the Greensand Way, here turn left uphill along the Greensand Way *(signed*

Leith Hill Tower). Continue up this broad stony track to arrive at the Tower on Leith Hill at TQ1396 4316.

At the tower do an about turn and walk back down the broad track. At the bottom of the dip at a junction of tracks turn left on a broad track *(the Greensand Way)* going downhill. After about 1km at a diagonal cross track continue on ahead. Later at farm buildings, on the right, continue on ahead. At an inverse Y-junction continue on in the same direction. Carry on the track *(GW)* ignoring others for a further 2.8kms *(1¾ miles)* to reach a junction with a lane.

Here turn right along a broad track. In 200m and where the track goes sharp right at TQ1316 4752 turn left over a step stile and carry on ahead. The track descends to meet another track at an inverse Y-junction at TQ1316 4775. Here turn left. After walking past a row of elevated houses reach an access lane. Here turn right and walk on through The Rookery along Rookery Drive. Just before reaching the A25 turn right on a track leading uphill.

At the Rookery

Photo L Ham

Keep to the obvious main track. At residences on the right go forward towards a lane. Cross the lane diagonally right and continue on the track opposite. Cross a grassy area in front of residences on the right and continue on the track ahead. The path meets or draws closer to the road on the right. Cross over the road diagonally left and continue on the track on the other side. The track descends to cross the terminal point of a road. Continue on the track opposite. Walk on behind residences and cross over a car parking area and go up the surfaced track in the right-hand corner. Go forward on a narrow enclosed track and go through a metal kissing gate and carry on ahead on a broader enclosed track. Later the track bears left downhill. Cross over a wooden footbridge over a stream to reach an access lane.

Here turn left and in 100m turn right up steps onto an enclosed track. Exit the track by a residence and continue along its access drive to reach a lane.

Continue on ahead in the same direction and at broad cross tracks turn right taking the left-hand of two tracks. In a few metres at a Y-junction fork left leaving the Greensand Way. In a few more metres bear left again and at a Y-junction bear left again. In a few metres cross over a broad cross track and go forward to enter the car park at Milton Heath.

Walk 6
Westcott, Park Farm, Abinger Roughs, Crossways Farm, Townhurst Wood, Abinger Common, Bushy Wood, The Wilderness, The Rookery

Map:	OS Explorer 146
Start/Finish points:	Village Green, Westcott at TQ1410 4860. (Parking in side roads by the church, avoid church activities)
Distance:	14kms (8¾ miles)
Time:	3½ hrs
Transport:	Rail: Dorking (then bus to Westcott) Bus: Westcott, The Rookery at the A25 road, Crossways Farm on the A25 road, Hollow Lane Wotton, Abinger Common.
Places of interest:	Westcott village, Samuel Wilberforce memorial stone, Crossways Farm, Tillingbourne, Wotton cottages, St James church and village stocks The Motte Abinger Common, The Rookery.
Refreshments:	*Prince of Wales ph, The Cricketers ph* Westcott, Shops In Westcott, *Abinger Hatch ph* Abinger Common
Local History Notes:	1, 2d, 4, 45, 55, 57, 61
Walk description:	Valleys, Woods, Lanes and Villages.

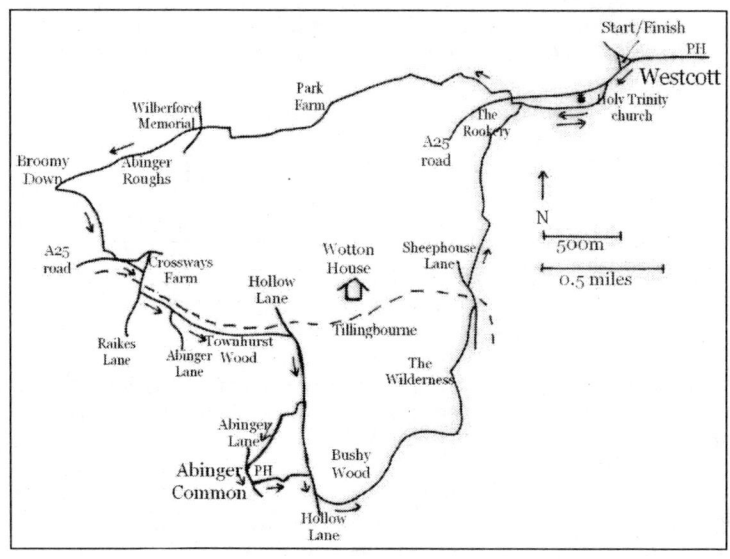

The route

Leaving the triangular village Green in Westcott walk west along the A25 and then bear left up the road immediately past the *Cricketers ph* which leads to the Parish church, Holy Trinity, Westcott. Walk on past the church and at the top of the rise notice the overflow church cemetery on the left. Opposite the cemetery and before a junction bear right on a track *(signed Greensand Way)*.

Westcott village   Photo L Ham

In a few metres notice one of two bench seats on the right in memory of those who were killed in the air raid on the 4th January 1944.

Soon cross a lane diagonally right to continue on a broad track. In 40m at a fork take the left track downhill. Maintain this downhill track to emerge at a road junction with Rookery Drive, the A25 Guildford Rd beyond.

Here turn right and cross over the A25 and turn left along it. Continue along Coast Hill and pass Balchins Lane and in just over a further 100m turn right up Coast Hill Lane. Before the entrance to Woodlands Cottage walk to the right of its access gate on an enclosed path. The path emerges at a junction of lanes here turn left.

Continue along a surfaced broad access drive. At a Y-junction bear right. Maintain this broad track emerging from a wooded area at a residence to fine valley views and the North Downs.

At a junction of tracks at Park Farm bear left and cross over the broad track diagonally left walking between old farm buildings. Continue on past a barn then on a narrower track. The track emerges at a road at TQ1125 4821.

Cross over the road diagonally left and continue on the track ahead entering Abinger Roughs. At TQ1105 4811 pass by a monument to Samuel Wilberforce. Maintain this broad track ignoring others for 900m to reach an open space of multi tracks at Broomy Down at TQ1027 4786. Here turn left across the open area and turn left again *(almost an about turn from the original track)* on a track at TQ1031 4783 on bearing 100 degrees. Maintain this grassy track

Walk 6   33

which swings right and downhill. Cross over a cross track and carry on ahead to reach a step stile at TQ1052 4775. Cross over the step stile and enter an irregular and hilly field. Cross the field ahead on bearing about 170 degrees on a faint track. Exit the field over a step stile and enter an area of private gardens and proceed on the track ahead. Exit the path at an access drive, here cross over it and continue on the track opposite to gain a road *(the A25)* at TQ1067 4738.

Cross over the road and go over a step stile by a gate and enter a field. Walk across the field on the right of two tracks on bearing about 125 degrees *(Crossways Farm buildings are on the left.)*. Exit the field over a step stile to gain a lane *(Raikes Lane)* here turn right.

In about 100m at a T-junction turn left along Abinger Lane. Pass by Abinger Mill *(now a private residence)*. In a further 50m where the lane goes right continue on ahead over a step stile and continue into the wooded area of Townhurst Wood alongside the Tillingbourne. Exit the track over a step stile at a lane *(Hollow Lane)*.

Here turn right and walk up the lane passing a row of detached cottages *(Wotton cottages)*. 15m beyond a bus stop bear right between two old gate posts on an access drive. Soon reach an open area and by-passing a gated and private entrance to Wotton Estate on the right reach the start of a single track. Follow this track as it leads uphill through a wooded area. At an inverse Y-junction continue on ahead alongside the perimeter fence of a school until it reaches the driveway just beyond a kissing gate. Carry on in the same direction and then left into the road leading from the school to reach a lane *(Abinger Lane)*.

Wilberforce Memorial, Abinger Roughs   Photo L Ham

Here turn left passing between *Abinger Hatch ph* on the left and St James church and village stocks on the right in Abinger Common. At the corner of the garden to *Abinger Hatch ph* turn left into a lane and follow it to its terminal point to re-join the sunken part of Hollow Lane. Here turn right and in less than 100m pass between two old gate posts to Wotton Estate *(marked Manor Gate)* and in a further 40m bear left up a sunken track.

Maintain the track ahead ignoring the cross track to a double gate and in a further 40m take the left of two tracks where it splits, *(it's the drier of the two)*. Soon the track bears left following a lane for about 100m. Where the track meets the lane continue on ahead following the lane.

Ignore the gated private entrance *(Mundies)* and bear left onto a broad track passing through the other entrance to Wotton Estate *(gate signed Pugs Corner)*. Maintain the surfaced access drive downhill and where it goes into a residence turn right on a track. Go over a step stile and cross a stone bridge over a dammed water course *(a tributary of the Tillingbourne)* and carry on up to a junction of tracks at TQ1260 4617. Go forward over a step stile and continue on up the steep track ahead towards Bushy Wood. At the top of the hill keep to the main grassy track following a left fence line. At a dip in the track and fork, turn left still following the fence line on bearing due north towards The Wilderness. At a very wide gate the path turns right still alongside the left fence line. Go forward down a narrower track which slowly descends to a step stile to reach a lane *(Sheephouse Lane)*.

Here turn left and in less than 100m cross over the Tillingbourne. And in a further 50m turn right up a track into a wooded area then cross diagonally left over an access drive and carry on the uphill track. At a cross track turn left. At a residence the track emerges at a lane *(Sheephouse Lane)* on a bend, here turn right on a broad track.

Where the track goes sharp right immediately past the corner turn left over a step stile. The track descends to meet a cross track here turn left. Exit the track at an access drive, here turn right and walk through the delightful settlement of The Rookery.

Exit the drive at the Rookery Lodge and before the A25 turn immediately right up a track. Keep to the main track leading uphill eventually reaching a lane.

Cross over the lane diagonally right and continue on the path opposite. Exit the path to regain the lane opposite the church cemetery, here turn left and walk down the lane. Pass by the church and walk down to the junction with the A25. Here turn right and walk into Westcott.

Walk 7
Friday Street, Wotton, North Downs Way, Westcott, The Rookery

Map:	OS Explorer 146
Start/Finish points:	Friday Street car park at TQ1258 4579.
Distance:	13kms (8 miles)
Time:	3½ hrs
Transport:	Rail: None on route
	Bus: Wotton, Westcott
Places of interest:	Friday Street, Wotton House, North Downs, Stowe Maries house Westcott, The Rookery, Tillingbourne.
Refreshments:	*Stephan Langton ph* Friday Street, *Wotton Hatch ph* Wotton, *Prince of Wales ph* Westcott, Shops in Westcott
Local History Notes:	26, 45, 57, 61
Walk description:	A hilly walk taking in villages, churches, woods and views.

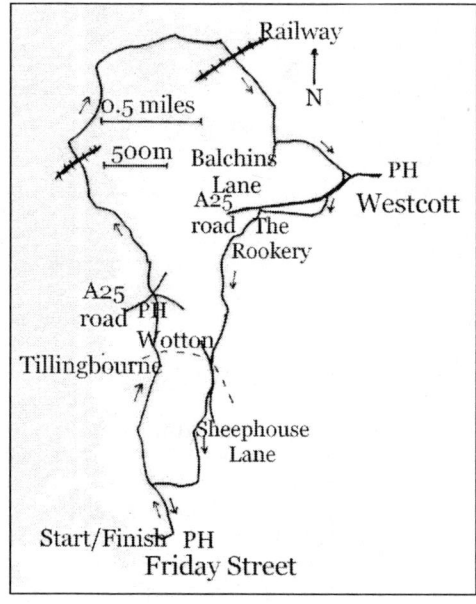

The route

Exit Friday Street car park in the left corner alongside the road on a track. Walk above the road on an elevated path alongside a fence. Go down steps and turn left to reach the road in a few metres, here turn right. In a few more metres reach a T-junction of lanes before the village pond. Here turn left down an access lane passing a cottage on the right. Soon cross over a shallow stream. Continue on down this broad track and at a cross

Track by a stone bridge, on the left at TQ1262 4619 (*the stream on the left is a tributary of the Tillingbourne*). Go over a step stile by a gate and carry on ahead on the enclosed broad track. At a Y-junction of tracks continue on ahead in the same direction. The track descends and does a short right and left then goes down shallow steps. The track becomes narrow round Wotton Estate. Go over a step stile and walk along the right-hand edge of a field (*Wotton House on the left*). Exit over a step stile to reach the access drive to Wotton House, here turn right.

In about 300m go over a step stile in the fence on the right and enter a field. Walk half-left across the field towards buildings on a faint track on bearing about 5 degrees. Exit over a step stile and go forward through a public house car park. Carry on down to a junction with Damphurst Lane and the A25 by *The Wotton Hatch* public house at TQ1262 4766.

The pond at Friday Street   Photo L Ham

Cross over the road and go down the narrow lane opposite (*signed The church of St John the Evangelist*). At the church at TQ1256 4794 turn left over a step stile into a field. Follow the church wall round to the right and at the corner of the churchyard follow the path which swings away to the left across a field on bearing about 320 degrees. On reaching the point of tree lines go over a step stile and forward on a narrow path in the same direction, then through a wooded area. Exit the wooded area over a step stile and continue on across a field. The path drops down to meet a junction of tracks at Park Farm at TQ1211 4838.

Take the broad track leading away in much the same direction on bearing about 340 degrees. Cross over a railway bridge and continue on ahead. Exit through a gate into a wooded area and ignoring the path on the right continue on the broader track uphill. At a Y-junction of tracks on a sharp bend at TQ1193 4889 take the left fork leading uphill. Meet a broad cross track (*North Downs Way*) by a gate and a pillbox at TQ1211 4934.

Walk 7

Here turn right and go through a gate and continue on the NDW. In about 200m at a Y-junction at White Downs take the right fork. After 700m at a cross track at TQ1275 4974 turn right downhill on bearing about 145 degrees leaving the NDW. After 300m at a T-junction of tracks turn left and in about 100m reach a 5 track junction at TQ1312 4969. Here turn right on a narrower track leading downhill on bearing about 160 degrees. Reach an active railway line at TQ1321 4956.

Cross over the railway line and continue on ahead. Where the track begins to go left at TQ1332 4945, turn right on a track through a tree line. Enter a field and follow the path round to the left passing through another tree line. Cross over a plank footbridge to enter another field. Continue along its left-hand edge and then go forward towards a tree line on the other side of the field. Exit the field over a step stile and enter a wooded area, carry on ahead. Go over a footbridge with step stiles at each end. Go forward over a third step stile to gain a lane *(Balchins Lane),* here turn left. *(The large house on the immediate right is Stowe Maries once the home of the actor Leslie Howard famous for his part in Gone with the Wind.)*

Stowe Maries, Westcott   Photo L Ham

At a T-junction with Westcott Street turn right along it. On approaching the triangular green in Westcott bear right and walk up to the A25 road. Here turn right along it and in about 100m cross over the road and turn left immediately past the *Cricketers* public house along Westcott Heath leading up to the church.

Walk on past the Parish church Holy Trinity, Westcott and at the top of the hill opposite the cemetery bear right on a track *(Greensand Way).* Walk on across a small green passing commemorative seats. Cross over a lane diagonally right and continue on the broad track on the other side. The track descends down a small gully and emerges at a T-junction with the A25 road opposite Rookery Lodge. Turn left along Rookery Drive.

Carry on past delightful cottages and just before entering a gate signed *(The Rookery)* take the path on the left beneath a row of residences. After 400m and at TQ 1315 4774 bear right up a steeper track. After the track levels out go over a step stile to reach a broad track. Cross over the track and go over the step stile opposite crossing a field slightly left on bearing about 200 degrees *(cutting the corner off the field)*. Exit the field over a step stile to gain a broad track *(Greensand Way)*. Here turn left and in 10m turn right to enter woodland. Follow a faint track downhill through the woodland, cross over an access drive diagonally left and continue downhill. The path meets a lane, here turn left.

In 50m cross over the Tillingbourne. In a further 100m bear right over a step stile to enter Wotton Estate. At the top of the rise at a junction of tracks continue on ahead on a broader track. At a track junction at the corner of a fence line follow the fence round to the right and continue on a broad grassy track. The path eventually goes steeply downhill and meets a junction of tracks before a stone bridge and a pond at TQ1261 4620, here turn left. At Yew Tree cottage take the right fork. Cross over a footbridge over a stream. Exit the track at a T-junction of roads opposite a pond at Friday Street.

Here turn right and cross over the lane to walk on the elevated path beside the lane. In less than 100m turn left up a track and in 5m turn right up steps. Walk alongside a right fence soon entering the Friday Street car park at TQ1258 4579.

Walk 8
Friday Street, Broadmoor, Tillingbourne spring, Coldharbour, Leith Hill Place, site of The Old Observatory

Map:	OS Explorer 146
Start/Finish points:	Friday Street car park at TQ1258 4579.
Distance:	14kms (8¾ miles)
Time:	3½ hrs
Transport:	Rail: none on route
	Bus: Coldharbour (infrequent)
Places of interest:	Friday Street, Broadmoor Tower, Tilling spring, Anstiebury Fort, Leith Hill, Leith Hill Place, Rhododendron Wood, The Old Observatory.
Refreshments:	*Stephen Langton ph* Friday Street, *The Plough Inn ph* Coldharbour.
Local History Notes:	3, 11, 19, 26, 32, 33, 34, 55
Walk description:	In the heart of the Surrey Hills, a hilly walk encompassing valleys, woods, Iron Age forts, hills, views and WWII history.

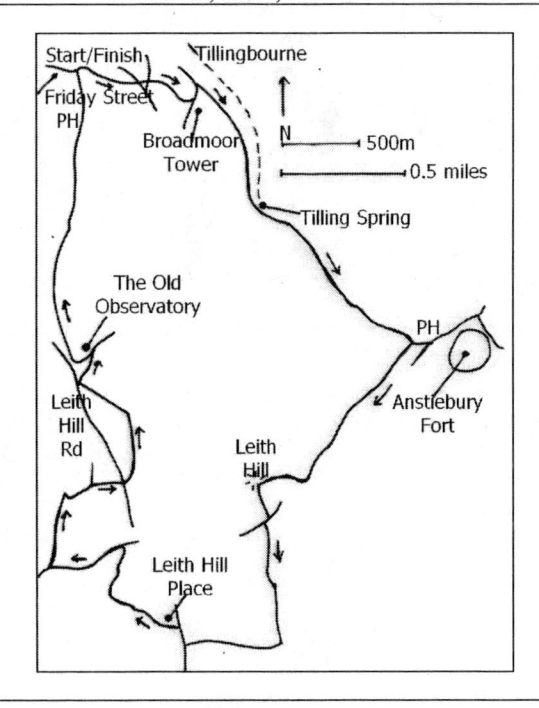

The route

Exit Friday Street car park in the corner by the road leading down to Friday Street. Walk alongside the road on an elevated path alongside a fence. Go down steps and turn left to reach the road in a few metres, here turn right. In less than 100m reach a T- junction before the village pond. Continue on ahead past the pond. Immediately just past the pond bear right through a gap in a fence line and take the path leading uphill into woodland. Maintain direction to reach a lane.

Cross over the lane diagonally right and continue on. In just over 100m cross over a second lane and continue on the track opposite.

At a Y-junction of tracks bear right. At an inverse Y-junction bear right downhill. Follow the track round to the left to reach a lane in Broadmoor village at TQ1348 4561, here turn left.

Walk on past residences in Broadmoor and in less than 200m turn right on a broad track, joining the Greensand Way.

Tilling Spring   Photo L Ham

At a Y-junction at TQ1389 4502 bear left leaving the Greensand Way. Walk by the idyllic Tilling Spring. Where the track goes left into residences go forward on a broad track into Duke's Warren. Keep to the main track ignoring others. At a multi track junction at TQ1457 4433 walk left a few metres through an earth banking and bear right on a broad track bearing about 160 degrees. In 20m bear left on a narrow track towards the woodland. In 40m cross over a narrow cross track and continue on ahead. Maintain this path to reach a broad cross track at TQ1478 4425 by a centrally positioned tree. Carry on ahead on bearing about 140 degrees. Maintain direction over the hill, the path then descends. Maintain the downhill track which joins or crosses over others. The track descends to a T-junction with a broad track. Here turn left and in 250m reach the village of Coldharbour.

Optional detour to Anstiebury Hill fort site: Facing The Plough Inn public house in Coldharbour walk left along the lane. After about 300m at a lane junction turn right and in about 100m reach an entrance area to the fort on the right. Return to Coldharbour village the same way.

Walk 8

Facing the *Plough Inn*, Coldharbour walk right and back up the track that you originally came down to the village, passing a telephone box on the left soon walking alongside a row of residences on a broad track. At a Y-junction take the right fork *(signed the Tower)*. Carry on up the track later pass Coldharbour cricket field on the right. After the cricket field, at a Y-junction, take the left fork. Maintain this broad obvious track ignoring others. When the track starts to go downhill meet a four track junction. Here turn right and in 10m take the right-hand fork downhill. The track descends to another multi track junction where it meets the Greensand Way, here turn left uphill along the Greensand Way *(signed Leith Hill Tower)*. Continue up this broad stony track to arrive at the Tower on Leith Hill at TQ1396 4316.

Continue on past the Tower downhill on a broad track to reach a notice board. Here turn left alongside a low fence line and walk round to the top of some steps. Turn left down the steps. At a track T-junction by a seat turn left downhill and then go down more steps to reach one of two car small parks at Windy Gap. Walk through the car park and gain the road. Turn right along the road and in 40m turn left into the second car park at Windy Gap.

Walk out of the back of Windy Gap car park *(which is within Leith Hill Place Wood)* on a track leading downhill in a southerly direction on bearing about 160 degrees. At a T-junction of tracks at TQ1396 4265 turn left. In less than 100m at a broad cross track at TQ1401 4260 cross over the track and continue on the narrower track opposite. Cross over a footbridge and emerge from the wooded area over a step stile to enter a field. Go forward on its right hand edge by a tree line. Where the tree line goes right continue on in the same direction due south. Once beyond a tall tree at the end of a tree line on the right at TQ1408 4220 turn right towards Hartshurst Farm buildings *(15th century, later 18th century)*.

Go over a step stile and walk on between the farm buildings on a broad farm track. After about 200m where the farm track swings right bear left on a short hard to spot track, which leads to a footbridge over a ditch. Then go over a step stile to enter a field. Here turn right. Follow the right-hand edge of the field to the corner go round the corner and in 20m turn right over a step stile. Go forward over a cross track and then go over a second step stile and continue on ahead on the right-hand edge of a field. Exit in top right-hand corner of the field through a kissing gate. Continue on in the same direction across a field. Exit in the right-hand corner over a step stile to gain a lane at TQ1347 4219, here turn right.

In less than 200m turn left over a step stile to enter Leith Hill Place. Walk on past a Ha Ha and past Leith Hill Place house on the right. Go over a step stile and continue on the track across a hilly irregular field. Exit over a step stile 10m to the right of a wide gate and continue on the track into woodland *(Leith Hill Wood)*. At a track junction bear right and join a broad sandy track on bearing about 300 degrees. Maintain this broad track which later goes right and uphill. At a Y-junction at TQ1293 4268 bear right. In 30m, cross over a cross track and continue on ahead. Maintain this track ignoring others to reach a cross track at TQ1311 4272, here turn left to reach the National Trust Rhododendron car park at TQ1311 4278 within the Rhododendron Wood.

Exit the car park to a lane *(Tanhurst Lane)*, here turn left. In about 100m and just before a Y-junction of roads turn right through a kissing gate to gain an enclosed track. Later go down steps and turn right. In 40m turn left up some steps. Continue on a winding track through woodland. At a T-junction of tracks at TQ1270 4309 turn right uphill. In 200m at a triangular junction at TQ1287 4319 meet the Greensand Way, here bear right and continue on the broad Greensand Way track leading slightly uphill. In just over 200m reach a road at Starveall Corner at TQ1309 4318.

Cross over the road half-right and in 10m leave the Greensand Way and turn left on a track on bearing about 20 degrees. At a broad cross track, *(Starveall car park on the left)*, continue on ahead. At diagonal cross tracks maintain direction. At a broad cross track at TQ1309 4365 turn left on bearing about 300 degrees. After almost 400m exit the track at a T-junction of lanes, here turn sharp right along a lane *(road signed to Broadmoor)*.

In 300m at TQ1290 4400 reach the entrance to The Old Observatory. Here do a sharp left turn on a track going back almost parallel to the lane. The track goes right then at an inverse Y-junction continue on downhill. *(The old fence line and banking round the Old Observatory site is still visible on the right).* At a cross track, at the corner of the Old Observatory site note the boundary stone on the right.

Optional detour: To view a second boundary stone and Azimuth pillar - Turn right and in about 100m reach TQ1276 4425, the boundary stone and pillar are on the right. Return to the track the same way.

Boundary stone and Azimuth pillar at The Old Observatory, Abinger

Photo's L Ham

Continue on down the track for a further 600m. Exit the track to reach a lane, continue on in the same direction and in about 100m, opposite St Johns' cottage, bear right on a broad track. Maintain this track ignoring others for

600m to reach the terminal point of an access lane. Go forward through Friday Street village and pass by the *Stephen Langton* public house to reach a T-junction by a pond.

Here turn left walk on the elevated path beside the lane. In less than 100m turn left up a track and in 5m turn right up steps. Walk alongside a fence on the right soon entering the Friday Street car park at TQ1258 4579.

Walk 9
Holmbury St Mary, Somerset Hill, Leith Hill, Abinger Bottom, Abinger Common

Map:	OS Explorer 146
Start/Finish points	Horsham Rd car park Holmbury St Mary at TQ1084 4509
Distance:	13kms (8 miles).
Time:	3½hrs.
Transport:	Rail: none on route Bus: Holmbury St Mary, Abinger Common.
Places of interest:	Holmbury St Mary, Leith Hill, Leith Hill Tower, Village well and Goddards Abinger Common.
Refreshments:	*Kings Head ph* Pitland Street, Leith Hill Tower *(weekends and bank holidays except xmas, plus Fridays 25 Mar 29 Oct, plus Wednesdays during August)*, Abinger Hatch ph, *Abinger Common (600m off route), Royal Oak ph* Holmbury St Mary
Local History Notes:	1, 30, 32, 34
Walk description:	Sandy paths which offer fine views of the Weald from Leith Hill. Woodland, hills and valleys feature along its route.

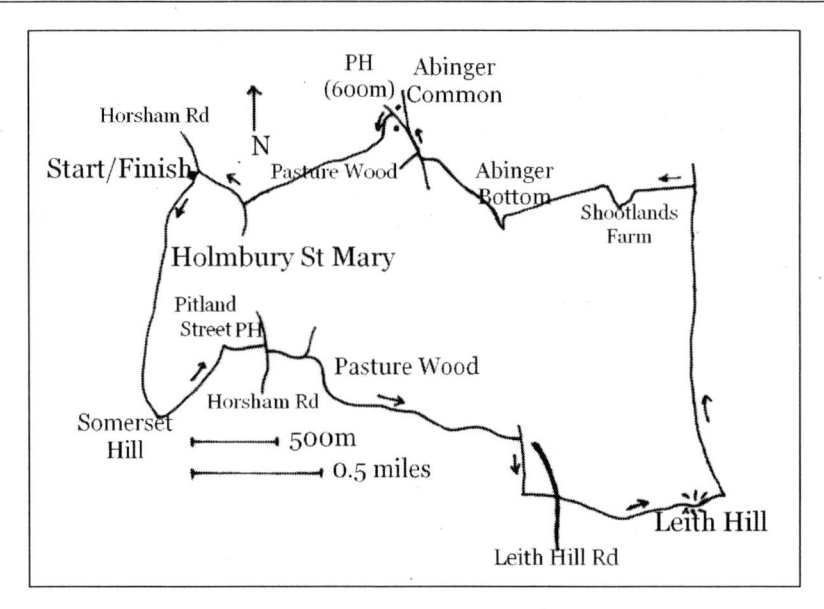

The route

Exit the car park on Horsham Rd, Holmbury St Mary at the back walking along the broad track leading away from the road. Maintain this broad track uphill for 1.7kms *(1 mile)* to reach a junction of several tracks. Here take the second exit on the left on a broad track on bearing about 50 degrees, which is the *Greensand Way*. After passing a sports field on the left, at a Y-junction follow the main path to the right going downhill. At a road *(Holmbury Hill Rd)* turn left and immediately fork right at a Y-junction. Go forward to reach a T-junction at Pitland St/B2126.

Here turn right and in 50m or less turn left along Pasturewood Rd. In just over 200m and where the road goes sharp left turn right on a broad track. Continue on this track for 1.3kms (¾ mile) to reach High Ashes Farm. Here carry on ahead on an access track to reach a T-junction of tracks. Here turn right and soon at a Y-junction continue on in the same direction. In a few more metres at a diagonal cross track continue on ahead. At a junction of tracks turn left. In just over 200m reach a road at Starveall Corner at TQ1309 4318.

Cross over the road half-right and continue on the broad track in much the same direction. Cross diagonally over a broad cross track and go forward on a narrower track uphill *(signed Footpath to Tower)*. Cross diagonally over a broad track and continue on uphill. Then joining a broad track continue on uphill to reach Leith Hill tower.

Walk on past the tower on the broad track leading downhill. At the bottom of the dip at a junction of tracks turn left on a broad track *(still the Greensand Way)* going downhill. After about 1km at a diagonal cross track continue on ahead. Later at farm buildings, on the right, continue on ahead. At an inverse Y-junction continue on in the same direction. In a further 130m at TQ1389 4512 leave the *Greensand Way* and turn left on a narrow track *(can be hard to spot)* leading uphill. At the top of the hill go over a step stile and walk across a small enclosure. Go through a gap in the fence and enter a field. Cross the field on the right-hand side by a fence. Go through a gate into another field and continue on ahead. Exit the field through a gate to go forward on a gravel access track past farm buildings *(Shootlands Farm)*.

Village well and Goddards, Abinger Common
Photo L Ham

Follow the farm access track round to the left and then turn right over a step stile and enter a wooded area. Bear left on a faint track leading downhill. At a cross track turn left, and in a few metres turn very sharp right. Eventually emerge from the wooded area at a lane.

Here turn right and in 25m turn left through a gap by a gate to enter a field. Walk on the left-hand side of the field. Exit the field in the left-hand corner through a wide gap in the hedgerow and go forward in the same direction to enter another field ignoring the gap on the left. Continue on the left-hand edge of the field. Before the end of the field bear left on a track to the left of tall trees. Pass between metal barriers and descend to an access track at residences at Abinger Bottom. Continue on ahead and in a few metres meet a lane on a bend.

Walk right for a few metres and take the footpath on the right leading downhill. Emerge over a plank bridge to a lane.

Here turn left and in a few metres turn right on a track leading uphill. In a few metres walk to the right of a small electricity compound and continue on behind residences *(on the right)*. The path broadens and goes left and uphill through a wooded area. Cross over a broad cross track and continue on in the same direction. Eventually emerge by residences at a lane.

Go forward along the lane in the same direction. Emerge at an offset road junction; here turn right along the road and in just over 100m bear left at a Y-junction on a road to Abinger Common. Pass by an ornate disused village well on the right and Goddard's on the left. In a further 100m by residences turn left on a path.

(For the Abinger Hatch ph continue along the lane for a further 600m).

At a cross track maintain direction walking uphill. Maintain the broad grassy track ahead ignoring all others. Where the track goes sharp right after 800m, go forward on a narrow track going steeply downhill. Exit through a gate to go forward on a short unmade road to reach a road *(Horsham Rd, B2126)*. Here turn right and in 300m arrive at the car park at Horsham Rd, Holmbury St Mary on the left.

Walk 10
Holmbury St Mary, Winterfold Hill, Raynards Hill, Duke of Kent school, Holmbury Hill Fort, Somerset Hill

Map:	OS Explorer 146 and 145
Start/Finish points:	Horsham Rd car park Holmbury St Mary at grid ref TQ1084 4509
Distance:	15.8kms (10 miles)
Time:	4 hrs
Transport:	Rail: None on route Bus: Holmbury St Mary, Duke of Kent School Ewhurst Rd
Places of interest:	Holmbury St Mary, St Mary's church Holmbury St Mary, Gasson Farm, Duke of Kent School, Winterfold Hill, Raynards Hill, Ewhurst windmill, Summerfold House, Pitch Hill, Holmbury Hill and Iron Age fort
Refreshments:	*The Royal Oak ph* Holmbury St Mary, *Windmill ph (Bar/restaurant)*, Pitch Hill (300m off route)
Local History Notes:	23, 27, 30, 31, 41, 44
Walk description:	Long sandy tracks, hills, spooky woods, many superb hilltop views.

Note: On this circular walk there are no refreshments on route after leaving Holmbury St Mary except for a bar/restaurant at Pitch Hill.

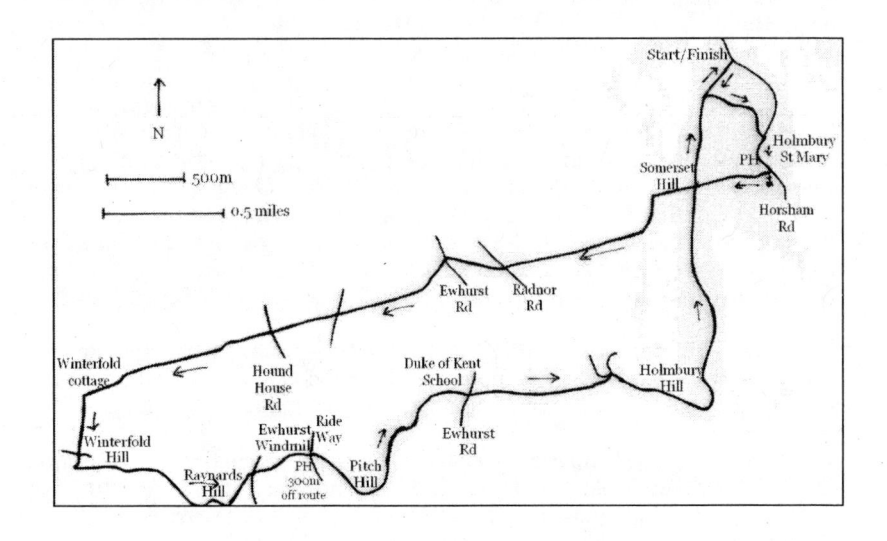

The route

Exit the rear of the car park on a broad track leading uphill. At a cross track after 260m at TQ1064 4490 turn left. Maintain this track ignoring others. Where the track begins to descend at a Y-junction take the left track downhill. The track emerges at a road by a telephone box.

Here turn right and follow the road round to the left skirting the triangular green and the *Royal Oak ph* at Holmbury St Mary. Just before St Mary's church turn right up a surfaced drive and continue past the church on a broad track which then goes right and meets a road junction.

Here turn left and in less than 100m turn right, initially on an access drive to residences. In 30m take the narrow track on the right leading uphill. At a cross track continue on ahead on the steep track opposite. At the top of the hill reach a junction of broad tracks at TQ1065 4437.

Continue on the broad track opposite. After 300m at a very broad cross track at TQ1036 4430 continue on a broad track leading downhill. The track descends to an inverse Y-junction at TQ1027 4418 continue on in the same direction on bearing about 200 degrees. At a 5 track junction at TQ1021 4406 take the second right track leading uphill between trees on bearing about 260 degrees. Maintain this broad track ignoring all others. In a small valley at TQ0952 4391 the track meets a broad cross track, continue on ahead on a narrower track. At TQ0939 4387 cross over another broad track and continue on in the same direction. The track meets a road *(Radnor Rd)* at TQ0927 4385

Cross over the road and continue on the track opposite. In 10m bear right at a Y-junction and in a few more metres turn right at a broader track. In less than 100m at TQ0919 4384, at a Y-junction, bear left on a track leading downhill through woodland. Cross diagonally over a cross track and continue on downhill. At the bottom of the hill turn left for 5m to reach a road *(Ewhurst Rd at Gasson Farm)* at TQ0889 4388.

Cross over the road and walk past Gasson Lodge soon bearing right on a broad track leading uphill. About halfway up the hill in less than 150m at TQ0874 4375 turn right up a very hard to spot track leading uphill into the trees soon gaining a shallow gully like track. The track emerges at a junction of tracks at TQ0866 4371. Continue on the track ahead across Hurt Wood on bearing about 250 degrees. In 150m at TQ0852 4367 cross over a broad cross track and continue on ahead. Maintain direction and cross over three further cross tracks, the path becoming narrower, and reach a road at TQ0813 4352.

Cross over the road and continue on the track opposite to reach a multi track junction at TQ0802 4357, here take the second left on a broad track on bearing 260 degrees. In a further 350m at TQ0768 4349 reach a road.

Cross over the road and continue on the track opposite in the same direction now entering Winterfold Wood. The track descends to a surfaced forestry track at TQ0752 4345 cross over the road and continue on the track slightly right through a more thickly wooded area. The track later descends to a cross track at TQ0730 4340, cross over the track and continue on the track

Walk 10

opposite. At the top of the hill meet a broad track at an inverse Y-junction at TQ0711 4335, continue on the broad track ahead in the same direction. In just over 100m at TQ0703 4334 where the broad track goes left continue on ahead take the right fork down a narrower track.

After negotiating a small valley re-join the broad track at TQ0692 4332, carry on ahead on the broad track. In less than 100m at broad cross tracks at TQ0685 4331 continue on head in the same direction. At a Y-junction at TQ0674 4328 bear right on a narrower track leading downhill. Pass by woodland barriers and reach a multi-track junction.

Go forward 20m to the centre of the first group of tracks and take the steep narrower track slightly right and uphill at about 305 degrees. Cross over a cross track and maintain direction. Cross over a cross track and then go forward a few metres and go over a step stile to reach a T-junction of tracks before Winterfold cottage at TQ0639 4314.

Here turn left and in a few metres take the right fork. At a cross track turn right and in less than 100m at a Y-junction bear left. Cross over a road and continue on the track opposite and so be rewarded with the magnificent unfolding view from Winterfold Hill at TQ0633 4270.

Here turn left along the Greensand Way. Maintain the track to a Y-junction by a Greensand Way marker on the right. Here bear left uphill to later reach a cross track. Cross over and continue through a wooded area on a faint track following Greensand Way marker posts to reach a lane at TQ0669 4263.

Here turn right and in less than 100m bear right on a track closest to the road still following the Greensand Way. In less than 200m at a junction of tracks turn right. In a few metres at a Y-junction take the left fork. At a T-junction at TQ0706 4239 turn right and follow the path round to the left. Maintain the track ahead ignoring others over Raynards Hill. Where the Greensand Way goes left at TQ0724 4231 you may bear right to gain a viewpoint.

Judge James seat at Raynards Hill   Photo L Ham

The Surrey Hills

From the viewpoint seat at Raynards Hill at TQ0731 4230 walk away from the view and re-join the broad Greensand Way track and turn right along it. The track descends to a car park by a road. Walk through the car park and exit to the road, here turn right. In a few metres reach a T-junction of roads.

Cross over the road and continue on the broad track opposite. Cross over two access drives *(to Summerfold House)* and continue on ahead. The track emerges to join a broad access track to a residence, continue on in the same direction along the broad track. Pass Ewhurst windmill and turn right. By the entrance to Four Winds residence bear left down a track. Exit the track and go forward to reach a road *(Ride Way)* at TQ0792 4265.

> For the Windmill ph *(Bar/restaurant)* Pitch Hill turn right down the road for 300m.

Cross over the road and go through the wide gates opposite. Immediately through the gates turn right on a track. Carry on this track to gain Pitch Hill at TQ0825 4233. Continue on past the trig point and further along there is a slight detour to a viewing area a few metres off the Greensand Way. Backtrack to the Greensand Way and continue on a downhill track by an intermittent right fence. At an inverse Y-junction continue on in the same direction on a broad track. Just past another view point bear right on a track leading downhill. At a surfaced access drive turn left and where it goes left into a residence continue on the broad track ahead. After about 200m at TQ0863 4287 leave the broad track at a Y-junction and bear right on a narrower track leading downhill. Go down steps crossing over a cross track, continue on down steps on the track opposite. Go through a kissing gate and enter The Duke of Kent School grounds. Exit the path to walk alongside playing fields and walk down to a road, here continue on in the same direction. Exit the school grounds by a lodge to gain a road *(Ewhurst Rd)*.

Cross over the road half-left and continue on an enclosed track. Go over a step stile and continue on ahead. Go through The McKinney kissing gate and carry on ahead. The track eventually merges with a broader track, continue on ahead in the same direction. At a T-junction of tracks turn left. At a Y-junction bear right. The track emerges at a road at TQ0979 4316.

Cross over the road and go forward up the access road to a car park. Walk on the right-hand side of the car park and turn right before the notice board and walk between two concrete bollards. Drop down and cross over a cross track and continue on the track opposite. Cross over a wheel chair friendly viewing area at TQ0994 4301 and continue on the track opposite. After 200m at a T-junction of tracks at TQ1014 4306 turn right. Maintain the track and direction and continue to Holmbury Hill fort viewing area at TQ1040 4294. Turn about from the view and exit the fort through the ramparts and walk downhill on the Greensand Way. Walk past a wooden barrier and in 20m at a Y-junction bear right downhill. At a junction of tracks at TQ1052 4313 bear right. Pass by wooden barriers and go forward on a broader track and in just over 100m at an inverse Y-junction continue on in the same direction. At a multi-track junction at TQ1058 4363 continue on the broad track ahead leading uphill and leaving the Greensand Way. Continue on this track ignoring others for 1.7kms *(just over 1 mile)* to reach the car park at Horsham Rd Holmbury St Mary.

Walk 11
Peaslake, Brook, Blackheath forest, Roman Temple, Dick's Hill

Map:	OS Explorer 145
Start/Finish points:	Pond Lane car park, Peaslake at TQ0863 4484
Distance:	12.5kms (7¾ miles)
Time:	3 hrs
Transport:	Rail: None on route
	Bus: Peaslake, Brook. Farley Green (All very infrequent),
Places of interest:	Peaslake, Site of Roman Temple Farley Heath, Site of Quaker burial grounds Peaslake, Quaker Orchard house Peaslake,
Refreshments:	*Hurtwood Inn* Peaslake, *William IV ph* Little London (400m off route)
Local History Notes:	25, 40
Walk description:	Undulating paths with valley views, villages, forest paths on sandy tracks.

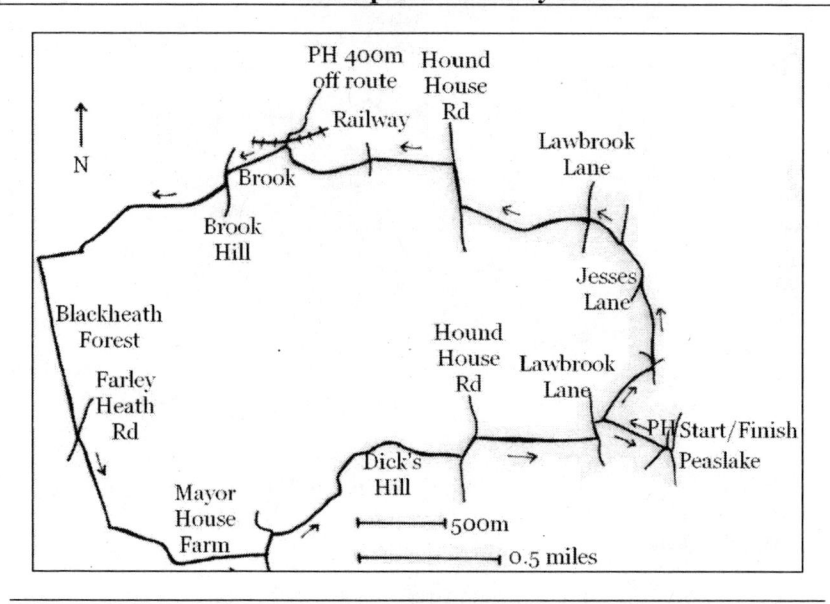

The route

Leave Pond Lane car park at TQ0863 4484 and turn right along Pond Lane to a T-junction in Peaslake *(Walking Bottom)*. Here turn right and walk past *Hurtwood Inn* then immediately bear right through a kissing gate on an enclosed path. Emerge to enter a field and continue along its right-hand edge. In the right-hand corner of the field, before its end, by a residence *(Quaker Orchard)* turn right over a step stile into a field. Continue down across the field. Exit over a step stile and enter another field walk along its right-hand edge. Follow the track round to the right and exit the field over a step stile by residences to gain a lane *(Pond Lane)*.

Here turn left and in a few metres at a T-junctions with Burchetts Hollow turn right at Burchetts Hollow and immediately turn left through a gap to enter a field. Continue across the field downhill on bearing about 360 degrees. At the very bottom of the field exit through a wide gate to gain a lane *(Jesses Lane)*.

Here turn right and after passing Oak Farm on the left and in a further 30m, turn left through a wide gate into a field soon crossing over a ditch keeping to the right-hand edge of the field. The path then slowly bears left. Exit through a kissing gate to gain a lane *(Lawbrook Lane)*.

Peaslake village stores   Photo L Ham

Cross over the lane and go past a gate and enter a field. Walk along the right-hand edge of the field. Exit in the right-hand corner and continue on an enclosed track. Emerge from the track at a road *(Hound House Rd)* at Cotterells Farm, here turn right.

In just over 200m and opposite Drydown Farm turn left through a gate and into a field. Continue on ahead across the field on bearing about 280 degrees. Exit the field through a gate and cross over a broad track, *(Ponds Lane)*. Continue on the enclosed track ahead. Exit over a step stile by the entrance to Ponds House and continue on ahead along its access drive. The access drive emerges at a T-junction by a railway arch. *(William IV public house 400m to the right.)*

Here turn left and walk along Brook Lane through Brook village. Exit Brook Lane at a T-Junction, here turn left.

Walk 11   53

In 70m bear right on a broad track. In 50m maintain the broad track to the right and enter a field system on bearing initially 230 degrees. In about 100m at a track junction bear right on a grassy track to the left of a tree line on bearing about 270 degrees. At the end of the tree line go forward and cross over a step stile on the left and continue on in the same direction up a field. Exit the field over a step stile to enter woodland at TQ0544 4609.

Go forward and in a few metres at a Y-junction take the left fork on a broad track at about 230 degrees. After 270m go over a step stile and continue on ahead and carry on downhill on a faint track. Go forward over a broad track and carry on a few metres to gain a second track by Lipscombe cottage at TQ0523 4584, here turn right on bearing about 270 degrees.

In about 250m at a residence continue on in the same direction. At a broad cross track at TQ0495 4580 turn left. At a cross track by a centrally positioned tree carry on ahead. Pass by Jelley's copse on the right and a residence, set back from the path, on the left. At a Y-junction at TQ0507 4517 bear left. Carry on ahead to gain a car park just before reaching a road *(Farley Heath Rd)* at TQ0516 4478.

| Optional detour left to view the site of a Roman Temple at TQ0517 4493. |

Cross over the road and take the right of two footpaths by a gate on bearing about 165 degrees. At a Y-junction take the left track by a fence line. At a diagonal cross track at TQ0533 4442 continue on ahead in the same direction. At a second and broader diagonal cross track at TQ0543 4431 continue on in the same direction on bearing about 140 degrees. At a small green triangulation at TQ0551 4423 turn left downhill. Meet and join a broad track, here bear left.

Plan of Roman Temple, Farley Heath   Photo L Ham

Continue on ahead and pass by Mayor House Farm buildings and carry on the track ahead. At a broad cross track *(Ride Lane)* at TQ0599 4411 cross over and continue on ahead. Continue on past residences and exit to a lane *(Row Lane)*, here turn left.

Where the lane goes sharp left turn sharp right down an enclosed track. At a cross track by a small pond continue on up the steep track opposite. At TQ0657 4437 cross over a surfaced forestry road and continue on the track opposite. In about 60m at a path junction take the left fork leading downhill, which becomes very steep at the bottom of the hill. Cross over a cross track and go forward up the track opposite and join an enclosed track and walk up to a step stile on the left. Go over the step stile and enter a field. Walk on in front of a residence. In about 100m turn right over a step stile by a gate and go forward to cross over another step stile to enter a field. Continue on the left-hand edge of the field. Exit in the left-hand corner of the field over a step stile and turn right on an enclosed track. Go over a step-stile by a gate and continue on ahead soon merging with a broader track, here continue on in the same direction. At a Y-junction of tracks take the right fork. The track emerges and joins an access drive to a residence, continue on in the same direction. The access drive emerges at a lane *(Hound House Rd)*.

Here turn left and in just over 100m turn right through a gate *(signed to Kiln Platt cottage)*. Once through the gate take the left-hand grassy track by the left fence. Exit the field through a gate to enter another field continue on the left-hand edge. Exit in the left-hand corner through a wide gate and go forward across another field. Continue on its access track to meet a lane, here turn left.

In just over 100m turn right at Quakers Orchard. Continue past the front of the residence and carry on a grassy track. Go through a broad gap where we re-meet the path from the outward journey earlier. Continue ahead walking along the left-hand edge of a field. Exit in the left-hand corner and walk down an enclosed track. Exit through a kissing gate to gain Peaslake village. Walk past the *Hurtwood Inn* and turn immediately left along Pond Lane to arrive at the car park.

Walk 12
Gomshall, Abinger Common, Sutton Abinger, Paddington Farm, Broomy Downs, Hackhurst Down, Netley Park

Map:	OS Explorer 145 and 146
Start/Finish points:	Gomshall railway station at TQ0880 4779
Distance:	14kms (8¾ miles)
Time:	3½ hrs
Transport:	Rail: Gomshall
	Bus: Gomshall, Abinger Common, Sutton Abinger, A25 at Paddington Farm
Places of interest:	Gomshall Mill, Motte Abinger Common, St James church and village stocks Abinger Common, Paddington Mill, West Hackhurst (*E.M. Forster's former house*).
Refreshments:	*Abinger Hatch ph* Abinger Common, *The Volunteer ph* Sutton Abinger, *The Compasses ph The Black Horse ph* Gomshall, Tea shops Gomshall, Gomshall Mill
Local History Notes:	1, 2, 29, 54, 55
Walk description:	A figure of eight walk taking in hills, views, ancient history, villages, country lanes and churches

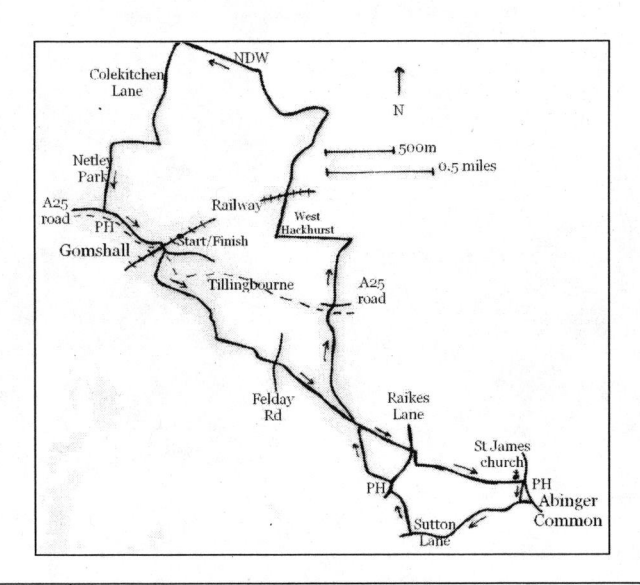

The route

From the station car park at Gomshall walk down the access road to the A25 road. Cross over the road and turn left through a pedestrian foot tunnel underneath the railway. On exiting turn right down a broad track

56 The Surrey Hills

(Wonham Way). Maintain this track and in 500m, at Southbrooks Farmhouse turn left on a track. Immediately after passing the farmhouse, at a Y-junction, bear right and follow a path up and across a field. Exit the field through a gap to gain a sunken track here turn right and in 60m turn left over a step stile to enter a field. Here turn right and walk along its right-hand edge. After 150m turn left by a finger post and walk across the field on a path on bearing about 100 degrees aiming to the right of a tree. Exit over a step stile and walk round the edge of a residence on an enclosed track. Exit the track to reach a road *(Felday Rd)*.

Cross over the road and go over a step stile. Go forward over a footbridge then on an enclosed track uphill. Ignore the step stile on the right and go over the step stile at the very top of the path to enter a field. Continue on ahead on a track following the line of telegraph poles on bearing about 120 degrees. Exit the field over a step stile and continue on the right-hand edge of a triangular hilly field. The track merges with another at TQ1020 4650. In about 150m at a track junction at TQ1029 4643 walk left through a tree line and carry on a broad track across a field on bearing about 120 degrees towards Raikes Farm. Exit the field at a lane *(Raikes Lane)*.

Here turn right and in 15m turn left through a kissing then bear right between the farm buildings. Walk on down a broad track passing Raikes Farmhouse on the right then in 40m at a track junction turn left. The track enters a field, continue on ahead. Exit in the neck of the field and continue on a narrow track alongside a hedgerow on the right. *(Soon notice the Motte on the right.)* Pass Abinger Manor on the right and exit the path through double metal gates to enter the churchyard of St James, Abinger. Walk through the churchyard to the right of St James church and exit through a lych-gate.

Village Stocks, Abinger Common   St James church, Abinger Common
                                                              Photo's L Ham

Here turn right alongside the churchyard wall. At the end of the churchyard wall continue on and descend to gain a lane *(Sutton Lane)*. Here turn right along the lane soon passing the entrance to Abinger Manor. At a triangular road junction bear right. In a further 350m reach a T-junction opposite *The Volunteer* public house at Sutton Abinger.

The Volunteer, Sutton Abinger   Photo L Ham

Here turn right up the lane and in 70m turn left on a broad track. Keep to the right of gates at a residence. After 400m reach a junction of tracks at TQ1029 4643 *(which we crossed earlier)*. Here bear left and walk in reverse along the track walked earlier. In about 150m at TQ1020 4650 at a Y-junction continue on ahead on this track going downhill which later becomes broader. At the bottom of the track go left and right and walk past Paddington Farm buildings. Go forward on a concrete access drive passing by Paddington Mill on the left and fish ponds on the right. Cross over the Tillingbourne and continue on up to the A25.

Cross over the road and go forward up the sunken track opposite. At the top of the track go through a gate and continue on the left-hand side of a hilly field. Exit the field through a gate and continue on up to T-junction at Broomy Downs at TQ1022 4783. Here turn sharp left on a broad track initially on bearing about 250 degrees. In 15m at a Y-junction keep to the right fork. Maintain this broad track which descends and goes sharp right, here go forward through a gate by a broad gate and carry on in the same direction on a narrower track. Exit the track through a gate and go forward a few metres to reach a lane *(Hackhurst Lane)*.

Walk half-right and go through a gate *(marked National Trust)* to the right of an access drive to a residence *(High Hackhurst, beyond is West Hackhurst once the home of E. M. Forster)*. Walk along the left-hand edge of a field towards Piney's Copse known locally sometimes as Forster's Wood. Exit the field though a gate and continue on through the copse. The narrow track eventually descends to meet a broad track at TQ0929 4784.

Here turn right and continue on underneath a railway arch. Maintain the broad stony chalk track slowly gaining altitude. Half way up the hill ignore a track on the left. Well before the top of the hill at TQ0940 4849 and before a fence on the left, turn left on a narrow track walking round a wooden barrier then walk alongside fence on the right and a hedgerow on the left. In 20m turn right through a kissing gate and walk through a wooded area to gain an open area at Hackhurst Down. Continue on a faint track uphill. Halfway up the track at TQ0943 4859 walk past or over a concrete and brick foundations of a WWII defence position. Continue on in the same direction up and over the hill then on a broader grassy track. Exit the track through a kissing gate by a wide gate to join the North Downs Way on a bend at TQ0950 4896.

Continue on ahead in the same direction initially alongside a fence on the left. At a T-junction of tracks, by a notice board, go forward through a kissing gate to join a broad track at TQ0949 4907 here turn left. In about 100m at an inverse Y-junction bear left on a broad track maintaining the North Downs Way. In a further 600m reach a multi-track junction at Gravelhill Gate by a concrete water tank on the right at TQ0890 4932. Here turn left on a narrower track *(known as Colekitchen Lane)* soon going downhill. Exit the path where a track goes into a farm, continue on ahead. Continue on past Cole Kitchen Farm and continue on its access drive. At an inverse Y-junction of lanes at TQ0875 4852 by a private drive turn right on a footpath to the right of a wide gate.

30m after passing a wide gate on the right reach a junction of tracks at TQ0838 4856 ignore the first track on the left and in 15m take the second track on the left. In 30m at a Y-junction bear left downhill. In less than 50m at a T-junction turn left downhill. Maintain the downhill track through woodland *(Netley Park)* drawing ever closer to the A25 road. Exit Netley Park down steps to reach the A25 in Gomshall diagonally opposite Queen St. Here turn left along the A25. Pass *The Compasses* public house. Continue on and just before the railway arch turn left up the access road to reach the railway station car park at Gomshall.

Walk 13
Shere, Newlands Corner, St Martha's Hill, Albury

Map:	OS Explorer 145
Start/Finish points:	Middle St, Shere at TQ0731 4780
Distance:	12.2kms (7½ miles)
Time:	3 hrs
Transport:	Rail: Gomshall *(1.5kms off route)*, then bus to Shere. Bus: Shere, Newlands Corner, Albury.
Places of interest:	The village of Shere, St James church Shere, The Barn Theatre Shere (disused), The White Horse ph, Tillingbourne, Village Well Shere, Newlands Corner, St Martha's Hill, St Martha's church and churchyard, Apostolic church Albury, The Ford Shere.
Refreshments:	*The White Horse ph, Prince of Wales ph,* Tea shops, Shere, Newlands Corner cafe.
Local History Notes:	5, 38, 49, 52, 55
Walk description:	Hills, broad level paths on top of hills, churches, stunning views from Newlands Corner and St Martha's Hill.

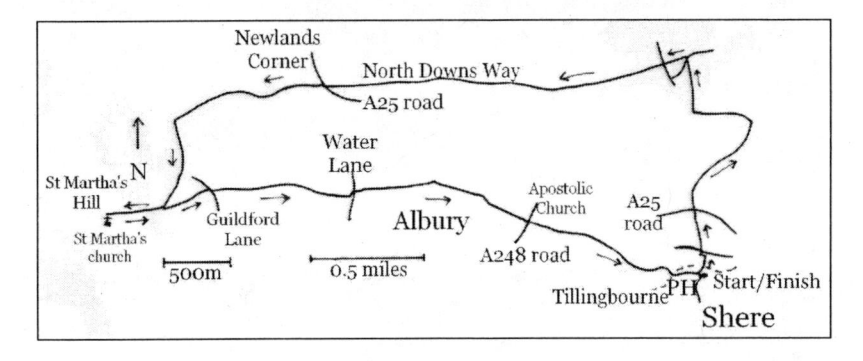

The route

Departing from Shere at Middle St by the Tillingbourne walk along Middle St to a T-junction by a disused well. Turn left into Upper St and in 30m turn right up a track passing a sports field. Proceed ahead soon going through a tunnel underneath the A25 road. Keeping to the main track and ignoring other tracks walk uphill for 800m *(Notice the WWII pillbox on the right)*. 100m after where the track levels out reach a cross track *(North Downs Way)* by a disused water tank at TQ0770 4890.

Village well, Shere
Photo L Ham

The Surrey Hills

Here turn left, later pass by a gate and stables at Hollister Farm. Continue on then follow the broad track round to the right at Hollister Cottage. In 130m ignore the track on the left and continue on ahead. At the next Y-junction at TQ0728 4919 take the right-hand fork. In a further 200m reach a road *(Coombe Lane)*.

Here turn right and in 30m turn sharp left on a track. In a further 200m reach a road *(Staple Lane)*.

Cross over and walk through the car park opposite *(West Hanger car park)* exiting on the far side on a track. Maintain the broad track ignoring all others. At a cross track at TQ0616 4920 continue on ahead. At a Y-junction continue on ahead in the same direction. Carry on ahead and reach a road *(A25)* at TQ0448 4920.

Albury Down   Photo L Ham

Cross over the busy road and continue on the path opposite bearing right towards the car park at Newlands Corner. Walk up to the refreshment bar at TQ0430 4927.

Walk south away from the refreshment bar across the car park and walk on down the hill veering right to join a track which swings to the right going west. *(The higher level track across Albury Down offers the better views.)*

At a Y-junction bear left slightly downhill. Soon cross over two angled cross tracks and continue on along the North Downs Way downhill into woodland. Continue down ignoring other tracks to reach a lane. Cross over the lane and go up the steps opposite and carry on ahead alongside the lane and a fence on the right. Exit the track and go through a gate on the left at a bend in the lane at TQ0339 4864 *(White Lane/Guildford Lane)*. Here turn right up a track passing double garages on the left. Continue on this uphill track ignoring all others. At the top of the track at a T-junction with a broad sandy track turn right. Carry on this uphill track to reach St Martha's church on St Martha's Hill.

Returning from St Martha's Hill initially back down the same path walked on the ascent passing the Downs Link at TQ0322 4837. Continue on ahead

Walk 13

and follow the broad sandy track past a WWIII pillbox then veer left down to a small car park. Walk past the notice board and bear right to walk along a path to a road *(Guildford Lane)* at TQ0335 4850.

Cross over the lane and go down the path opposite on bearing about 90 degrees. After 600m go over a cross track and through the gate opposite and into a field. Cross the field half-right going uphill on bearing about 110 degrees. Exit through a gate and go down a path by a wood. Descend to an access lane, here turn left and in 10m turn right.

Soon pass by a residence and in a further 600m at a junction of tracks by a residence turn right to pass in front of a residence. Beyond it go over a step stile by a gate and continue on ahead. In 150m at a Y-junction take the right-hand path leading slightly uphill. This enclosed path goes round the edge of an unseen quarry. Cross over its access road and carry on ahead. Go over a step stile by a gate and into a field. Cross the field keeping to the left-hand edge. Cross over a step stile by a gate, then go over a brook and then over a second step stile to reach a road *(Albury Rd, A248)* at TQ0599 4825. *(To the right is the Apostolic church.)*

Apostolic church, Albury   Photo L Ham

Cross over the road and go forward up the track opposite. Go through kissing gate by a gate and into a field. Continue ahead on bearing about 120 degrees to join the point of a fence. Carry on ahead alongside it in the same direction. Exit over a step stile by a gate and enter Silver Wood. Exit the wood at a kissing gate and cross a field in the same direction. Exit the field through a metal kissing gate and go into a wooded area. Descend to a lane, cross it and continue on the path opposite. Descend between residences to a lane where turn right. In 150m cross over a footbridge at a ford and follow the lane round to the left and along Lower St to a T-junction with Middle St at Shere.

Lower St, Shere   Photo L Ham

Walk 14
Shere, Gomshall, Peaslake, Farley Green, Brook, Little London

Map:	OS Explorer 145
Start/Finish points:	Middle St, Shere at TQ0731 4780.
Distance:	13kms (8 miles)
Time:	3½ hrs
Transport:	Rail: Gomshall
	Bus: Shere, Gomshall, (Peaslake, Farley Green, infrequent)
Places of interest:	Shere village, St James church Shere, Shere museum, Gomshall Mill, Peaslake village, Quaker Orchard Peaslake.
Refreshments:	*The White Horse ph, Prince of Wales*, Shops and tea shops, Shere, *The Black Horse ph, The Compasses ph,* Gomshall Mill, Gomshall, *Hurtwood Inn ph* and shops Peaslake
Local History Notes:	29, 40, 49, 55
Walk description:	Undulating paths and a gentle climb to Peaslake offering valley views amidst hills and villages.

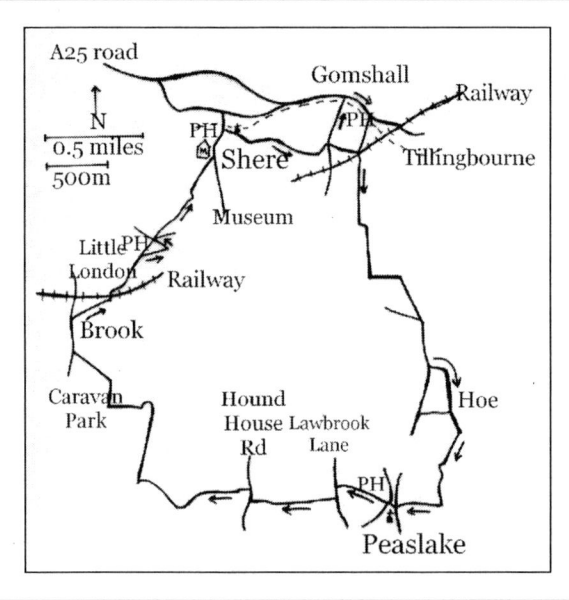

The route

With your back to the *White Horse* public house in Shere walk along the lane opposite towards the church. Enter the churchyard and walk round to the left *(notice Anchoress plaque on church wall)*. Beyond

Walk 14

the church turn right to exit through a gate to a lane. Here turn right back towards the village for a few metres. Then turn sharp left to go through a gate onto an enclosed path leading uphill. Exit through a kissing gate and immediately reach a junction of paths, here turn left. At a T-junction of tracks by residences turn left down an access track. Exit Gravelpits Lane at a junction of lanes. Here turn left down the lane *(Queen St)* and continue to a T-junction with the A25.

Gomshall Mill, Gomshall   Photo L Ham

Here turn right and walk through Gomshall. In 300m turn right before Gomshall Mill along Goose Green crossing over the Tillingbourne. Where the lane goes sharp right turn left into Tower Hill walking through a railway arch. On exiting take the footpath on the right-hand side of the road in front of residences. Exit the footpath where the lane goes sharp right. Cross over the lane and go forward in the same direction up the footpath opposite.

Plaque at St James' church, Sheer

Outline of Anchoress's enclosure
St James' church, Shere
Photos L Ham

At a T-junction of tracks turn left. At another T-junction of tracks turn left. After 280m turn right along a track alongside a wooden residential fence on the left. Maintain direction on this enclosed path between residences crossing over access drives. Emerge from the track to walk forward along Wonham Way for 40m to reach a road.

Here turn left into Hoe. After 500m turn left along Hoe Lane. Where the lane starts to descend and go sharp right, continue on ahead along Franksfield. After 200m at a Y-junction bear right and ignoring the track on the right continue on the broad track ahead. Maintain the track past residences and at its terminal point go forward through a gap into a wooded area on a narrow track. At a Y-junction bear right downhill soon reaching a surfaced access lane, here turn left.

Presently reach a small car park at Colman's Hill. Just by the car park take the right of two tracks going away from the car park passing by a bar gate on a broad track leading uphill. At a Y-junction of tracks take the right fork on the narrower track leading uphill. At a cross track at TQ0914 4472 turn right on bearing about 270 degrees leading uphill. At a junction of tracks go forward through wooden barriers at TQ0902 4473 and proceed on an enclosed track. Go past a second barrier and continue on ahead. Walk down a surfaced access lane. At a T-junction cross over the lane and go through a barrier and continue on a track downhill. Descend to a lane *(Radnor Rd)* and turn right into the village.

Walk past the front of *Hurtwood Inn* and immediately turn right through a kissing gate on an enclosed track leading uphill emerging to walk along the right-hand edge of a field. In the right-hand corner go through the gap and go forward past a residence and continue down its access drive to reach a lane.

Here turn left. In about 100m turn right on a track, *(a sign on the gate reads Peaslake Recreational Ground).* Walk on between fields exiting through a wide gate, continue on the right-hand side of another field. Exit in a dip in the right-hand corner of the field and continue on ahead on the right-hand edge of another field. Exit the field in the right-hand corner through a wide gate to reach a lane at the entrance to Kiln Platt cottage.

Hurtwood Inn, Peaslake   Photo L Ham

Here turn right and in 120m turn left by the entrance gate to Hound House on a broad wheel surfaced track. The track goes left and right. Go through a wide gate and continue on the grassy track ahead. Later walk to the left of a fence in front of a residence. At a junction of tracks continue on ahead in the same direction on a narrower track. At an inverse Y-junction continue on in the same direction. In less than 100m at a Y-junction take the right-hand fork. Exit through a wide gate and walk on between farm buildings, continue on

Walk 14

down its access track. Go through a wide gate and meet a cross track, here turn right at Lockhurst Hatch Farm at TQ0656 4497.

After 600m and where the track goes into Dilton Farm, continue on in the same direction on an unsurfaced broad track. In a few metres turn left over a step stile and follow the enclosed path for 450m to reach a path on the right before a kissing gate into a caravan park. Here turn right on the path and walk alongside the caravan park. Exit the path through a gate and go forward between farm buildings and an enclosed duck pond. Go through a kissing gate and enter a small field crossing it half-left on bearing about 320 degrees. Exit over a step stile and go forward across another field in much the same direction. Exit over a step stile over a double fence line and continue in the same direction across another field. Exit over a step stile and cross over a broad track and continue down the track opposite. Exit the path and re-gain the lane *(Brook Hill)* here turn right along it.

In 150m turn right into Brook Lane *(road signed Shere Peaslake)*. Follow the road underneath a railway arch and carry on into Little London. Just past the *William IV* public house bear right on a track. After 300m, at a junction of tracks, turn left. In a further 100m meet a road at a triangular junction.

Ramblers in the Surrey Hills   Photo L Ham

Here cross over the road and continue on the track opposite veering right almost immediately. The path becomes more defined. At a diagonal cross track carry on in the same direction. At a Y-junction continue on in the same direction. Maintain this downhill sunken track ignoring two inverse Y-junctions. In a further 40m at a Y-junction take the right-hand fork going uphill for a few metres then descending, eventually reaching a surfaced access road. Continue on ahead in the same direction. Exit the access road *(Pathfields)* at a T-junction with Shere Lane. Here turn left and pass by Shere museum on the left and soon arrive at Middle St in Shere.

Walk 15
Newlands Corner, Albury, Blackheath forest, Farley Green, Brook, Albury Estate, Silent Pool, North Downs

Map:	OS Explorer 145
Start/Finish points:	Newlands Corner car park on the A25 at TQ0433 4924.
Distance:	13.5kms (8½ miles)
Time:	3½ hrs
Transport:	Rail: None on route
	Bus: Newlands Corner, Albury, Farley Green (infrequent), Silent Pool (A25)
Places of interest:	Newlands corner, Albury village, Montgomery cairn Albury cricket ground, Old Saxon church Albury Estate, Catholic Apostolic church, Albury, Sherbourne pond, Silent Pool, WWII pillboxes.
Refreshments:	Newlands Corner cafe, *Drummond Arms ph*, Albury, *William IV ph* Little London (400m off route)
Local History Notes:	5, 6, 7, 9, 25, 38, 50, 55
Walk description:	A hilly walk either side of the Tillingbourne valley from the chalk hills of the North Downs to the greensand of Blackheath common offering hills, views, villages, forests, parkland, churches, ponds and WWII history.

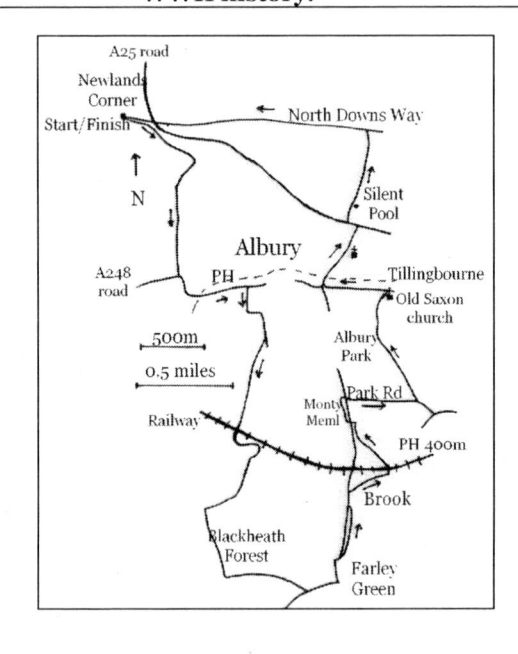

Walk 15

The route

Walk out of the car park in an eastbound direction back towards the A25 road. Before the road bear right on a track and in a few metres meet a broad cross track also from the car park. Here turn right downhill initially on bearing about 160 degrees on a broad gravelled track. At a track junction by a WWII pillbox bear right maintaining the broad track. The track meets another broad track on a bend, continue on ahead downhill. After 200m at another junction of tracks continue on ahead in the same direction now on a surfaced access lane *(Water Lane)*. Exit Water Lane at a road T-junction *(the A248)*.

A painter at Newlands Corner   Photo L Ham

Village shop, Albury   Photo L Ham

Cross over the road and turn left along the raised footpath. Enter Albury village ideally crossing over to the other side of the road at the bridge over the Tillingbourne. Pass by the *Drummond Arms* public house and continue on through Albury.

Just past Albury house on the right turn right up an enclosed surfaced footpath. Exit the path up shallow steps and turn left on a track.

At a junction of tracks on a bend at TQ0537 4769 keep to the right-hand sunken track uphill. At a Y-junction of tracks at TQ0536 4748 bear right into woodland soon walking alongside a fence on the right. At a broad cross track at TQ0529 4733 continue on ahead now going slightly downhill. In a further 200m cross over a cross track and continue on ahead. Exit the woodland over a step stile at TQ0521 4709 and enter a field, here turn left. Soon exiting the neck of the field walk on in the same direction on a very faint track on bearing about 190 degrees aiming to the left of two/three trees. Exit the field across an active railway line at TQ0514 4676.

Not The Old Pharmacy, Albury   Photo L Ham

Exit the railway crossing to enter another field. Continue on ahead and walk between tree lines. Go through a wide metal gate and walk on past a cottage. Exit through a wide gate and continue on ahead through Ford farm. At a T-junction of tracks at TQ0536 4658 turn right.

At a Y-junction of tracks at TQ0513 4624 continue on ahead. Exit this gully track at a multi track junction at TQ0499 4618. Continue on the broad track ahead on bearing about 290 degrees. In less than 200m at TQ0480 4617 at a cross track turn left on bearing about 170 degrees.

Continue on this track ignoring all cross tracks. Later the track narrows to a gully and goes downhill and then broadens again. At a junction of tracks at TQ0499 4555 turn left by a centrally positioned tree.

In 20m at a Y-junction take the left fork on bearing about 70 degrees. At TQ0545 4557 the track merges with an access track to two residences, continue on ahead in the same direction on the broad access track. The track emerges at a road *(Farley Heath Rd)* at TQ0569 4546, here turn left.

Walk on past Farley Heath Green on August Lane and continue into Brook Hill. In about 100m and just past the entrance to Edgeley Holiday Park bear right on an enclosed track. Exit the track to regain the road briefly and in 20m take the broad track on the right and pass by a wide gate. Continue on ahead parallel to the road. Where the broad track goes right at a gate go left on a narrower track downhill. Exit the track and regain the road again, here turn right along it.

Walk 15

At a T-junction of lanes turn right along Brook Lane and walk through Brook village. Pass underneath the railway arch and turn sharp left on a track.

(For the William IV public house continue along the lane for 400m).

Emerge at a cottage and go forward on its access drive and continue on ahead. In about 250m at a broad access track at TQ0615 4668 turn left. Soon reach a lane, cross over the lane diagonally right and continue on the track. In 20m at a Y-junction take the right-fork and keep parallel to the road. Eventually gain Albury Cricket Ground, continue on its right-hand edge. In a few metres on the right notice the stone cairn at TQ0600 4690:

> From this spot in May 1944
> Field-Marshal Sir Bernard Montgomery
> (Monty)
> addressed Canadian troops
> prior to the D-Day landing.

Continue on round the edge of the field exiting through the car park to take the right fork to reach opposite a T-junction of roads.

Cross over the road diagonally right and go forward along Park Rd walking along its possible grass verge. Where the road goes right, turn left on the left of two tracks going through a metal gate to enter Albury Park at TQ0657 4701. Pass by a cottage and go through a second gate and continue on ahead soon going left and right. Cross over a broad cross track and continue on ahead. The track later descends, cross over a cross track and continue on downhill. Near the bottom of the hill at a Y-junction take the right fork. Exit through a kissing gate and go forward to meet an access drive.

A very silent – Silent Pool – during a drought 2006

Photo L Ham

Cross over the access drive and walk slightly right to reach the Old Saxon Church. At the churchyard gate do an about turn and walk back to regain the access drive. Walk along it away from the church on bearing about 270 degrees *(on the right is the Tillingbourne)*. Exit through the entrance gate to gain New Rd, here turn right and in 30m at a T-junction with the A248 turn right along it.

Walk over a bridge over the Tillingbourne and past the Catholic Apostolic church on the right. At a T-junction with the A25 turn left along it. In about 100m turn right and cross over this dual carriageway.

Walk to the right of the Silent Pool and Sherbourne Pond car park and continue on the broad track ahead. In less than 100m pass by Sherbourne Pond on the right and carry on the broad track alongside it. Continue on up to Silent Pool there are paths on either side of it to the top end. At the top end of the pool exit up the steep steps to gain a track taking the left fork and soon at a T-junction of tracks turn right uphill. Proceed on the uphill track passing a WWII pillbox on the right. At the top of the hill meet a cross track, the North Downs Way at TQ0613 4915, here turn left.

Maintain this track and after 1.8kms *(just over 1 mile)* reach the A25 road at TQ0449 4920. Cross over the busy road and bear right and walk up to the car park at Newlands Corner.

Walk 16
Blackheath, Blackheath Forest, Farley Green, Albury Park, Albury

Map:	OS Explorer 145
Start/Finish points:	Blackheath Common car park near Blackheath village at TQ0363 4621
Distance:	12kms (7½ miles)
Time:	3 hrs
Transport:	Rail: Chilworth (1.6kms off route, 1 mile) Bus: Chilworth (1.6kms off route, 1 mile), Farley Green (infrequent) and Albury
Places of interest:	Albury village, Albury Park, Old Saxon church Albury Park, Apostolic church Albury
Refreshments:	*The Villagers ph* Blackheath, *The Drummond Arms ph* Albury (250m off route), *William IV ph* Little London (300m off route)
Local History Notes:	5, 6, 7. 9, 25,
Walk description:	Forests, farms, lanes, villages and parkland. Mainly flat some undulations.

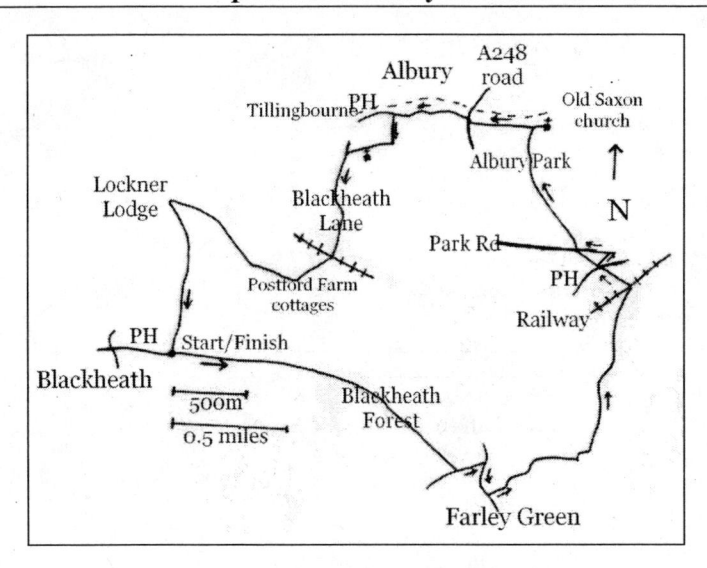

The route

Depart from the car park at Blackheath Common at TQ0363 4621 exiting through the back of the car park on a broad track on bearing about 80 degrees. Continue on in the same direction for 1.3kms *(¾ mile)* to reach TQ0490 4612. Here follow the track bearing right and at a junction of tracks at TQ0502 4602 continue on ahead on a broad sandy bridleway. At an inverse Y-junction at TQ0515 4595 pass by a seat. Continue on ahead, the path veers to the right and begins to go downhill. At a broad cross track by a residence at TQ0526 4583 turn left. Maintain the broad track ignoring all others for 440m to arrive at a road *(Farley Heath Rd)* in Farley Green at TQ0570 4547, here turn left.

In 150m and just before the village green turn right on a broad track alongside the Green. At the other side of the Green join the road, here turn right along it. Just past Medlar cottage, on the left, turn left on an enclosed path. Go through a kissing gate and enter a field. Cross the field diagonally left and exit in the top left-hand corner through a kissing gate. Continue on an enclosed path round the edge of a field. Exit through a kissing gate to enter Edgeley Caravan Park.

In a few metres turn right to join an access drive on a bend. Continue on in the same direction along the access drive going uphill. Follow the road round to the left and continue on. Where the road goes left again turn right on a short road. In a few metres turn right again and in 10m turn left on an enclosed path to emerge down steps to another access drive, here turn right. In 20m bear left on a track to exit the caravan park through a kissing gate.

In a few metres at a junction of tracks at TQ0633 4557 continue on in the same direction on bearing about 90 degrees. Follow this track and exit over a step stile at a junction with a cross track called Ponds Lane at TQ0668 4560, here turn left.

Continue along Ponds Lane for 1.2kms (¾ mile) eventually reaching a railway crossing by residences at TQ0698 4678. Cross over the active railway and continue on the track ahead to reach a road junction at TQ0675 4690. Cross over the road and take the footpath opposite leading into a wooded area. At an inverse Y-junction at TQ0680 4699 turn sharp left on a broad track. The path later draws close to the road we crossed previously and emerges at a junction of paths by a Lodge *(South Lodge)* at TQ0657 4701.

Albury Park   Photo L Ham

Here turn right through metal gates into Albury Estate and Albury Park. Walk on past the Lodge and in about 150m go left and right then maintain direction. Keep to the signed tracks through this private estate. At a cross track continue on in the same direction. The track begins to descend and towards the bottom at a Y-junction take the right-hand fork. Soon exit through a kissing gate and go forward down to reach an access drive. Cross over the access drive and walk slightly right to reach the Old Saxon church. At the churchyard gate do an about turn and walk back to regain the access drive. *(on the right is the Tillingbourne)*. Walk along the drive or grass verge away from the church on bearing about 270 degrees to reach the gate by the Lodge at New Rd.

Exit the gates and turn right. In 25m meet a road *(A248)* on a bend at TQ0576 4790. *(Nearby further along the A248 to the right is the Apostolic Church).*

Here turn left *(signed Albury, Chilton)* and walk along an elevated path alongside the road. The path descends to road level; continue on the footpath ahead towards Albury. Just past the fishing pond on the right and at TQ0524 4791 turn left up an enclosed surfaced footpath. Exit the path up shallow steps and meet the terminal point of a lane, here turn right.

Continue on past the parish church of St Peter and St Paul Albury. Where the lane turns sharp right, turn left along Blackheath Lane. After 500m and at the top of the hill where a broad track comes in from the left, take the enclosed footpath on the right that runs parallel to the lane ahead. Cross over an active railway line and then walk half-right across a field. Exit over a step stile to join a farm access drive. Here turn right and continue on past the farm house and go over a step stile and carry on a broad unsurfaced track to the left of a tree line. Go over two step stiles in a tree line and enter a field. Cross the field on a faint track on bearing about 300 degrees. Exit over a step stile and drop down and continue on an enclosed broad grassy track. Exit through a gate by a Lodge *(Lockner Lodge)* at a lane.

Cross over the lane and turn very sharp left on a path *(Downs Link)*. Exit the path after 750m by a residence at a lane. Go forward on the broader path to the left of the Downs Link path and enter a wooded area. At a Y-junction bear right and walk on to meet a road.

Here turn right and in 30m turn left on a track. In just over 100m arrive at the car park at Blackheath Common at TQ0363 4621.

Walk 17
Pewley Down, St Martha's Hill, Waterloo Pond, Blackheath, Wonersh Common, Chinthurst Hill, East Shalford

Map:	OS Explorer 145
Start/Finish points:	North Downs car park Pilgrims Way/Echo Pit Rd, Guildford at TQ0036 4839
Distance:	16kms (10 miles)
Time:	4½ hrs
Transport:	Rail: Guildford 2kms off route, then bus to Shalford Rd/Pilgrims Way at Shalford Park, Shalford then bus as above
	Bus: Guildford Shalford Rd/Pilgrims Way
Places of interest:	Pewley Down, St Martha's church, Waterloo Pond, Chinthurst Hill
Refreshments:	*The Villagers ph* Blackheath (300m off route), *The Seahorse Inn ph* Shalford (300m off route)
Local History Notes:	9, 18, 47, 48, 52, 55, 60
Walk description:	A hilly walk taking in mills, ponds, a hilltop church and many stunning views.

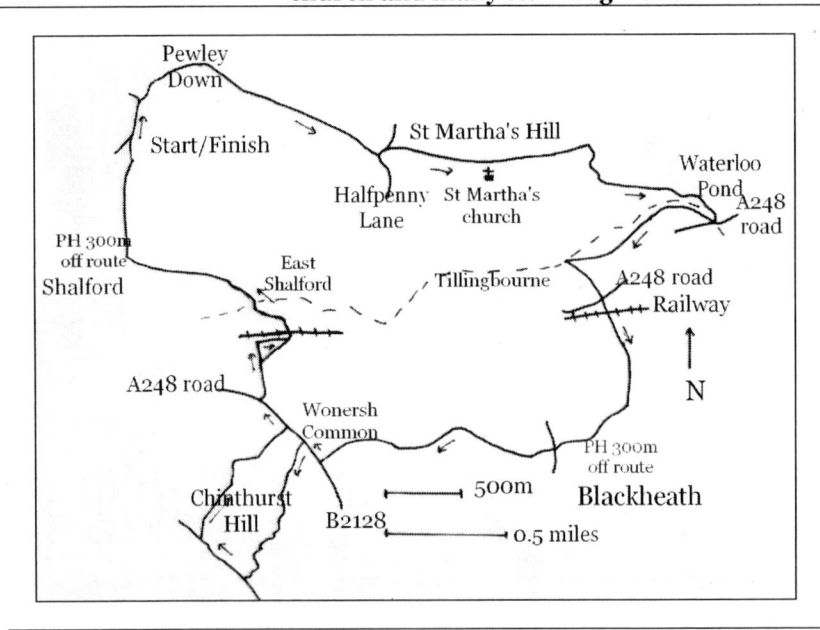

The route

From the North Downs Way car park off Pilgrims Way/Echo Pit Rd at TQ0037 4839 gain the bank at the back of the car park and turn left on a broad track. Soon reaching a road *(Echo Pit Rd)*, here turn right. Where the road goes sharp left continue forward on Northdown Lane, a surfaced public bridleway. Where it goes right in front of residences continue on a narrower enclosed track leading uphill soon bearing half left on an obvious track up the hill. At the top of the hill at a T-junction of tracks turn right. And so reach Pewley Down at TQ0075 4897.

Continue on past the concrete marker stone. In about 150m and just before a hedgerow bear right on a track leading downhill to the right of the hedgerow. Enter a wooded area and later at a T-junction turn left. Follow path bearing right and carry on ahead on an enclosed path to exit Pewley Down at a junction of tracks at TQ0178 4856. Cross over the broad track and go forward on the track opposite into a wooded area. The path soon divides into bridleway and footpath. At a cross track turn left along the North Downs Way and in 100m reach Halfpenny Lane at TQ0206 4837, here turn left. In 25m by Southernway Cottage turn right on a track. Continue on the sandy track ahead which goes up St Martha's hill eventually reaching St Martha's church. *(Notice the grave of Bernard Freyberg VC.)*

St Martha's church, St Martha's Hill   Photo L Ham

Walk on through St Martha's churchyard exiting through a gate *(notice commemorative stone by the gate to Yvonne Arnaud)* and keep on ahead downhill later passing a notice board on right *(Downs Link)* and a WWII pillbox on the left. Keep right at all junctions to reach a clearing, here turn right at TQ0352 4843 going downhill. In a few metres at an inverse Y-junction bear right downhill. At a T-junction of tracks before a fenced hilly field turn left. Maintain this undulating path through woodland above waters. The path eventually descends to join an access lane by a residence and a pond *(Waterloo Pond)*. At this junction turn immediately left on another track. Continue on and go over a step stile and enter the garden of a residence. Walk on past their greenhouse and across their lawns on a paved path and past the front of their house. Continue on along a driveway passing cottages. On

The Surrey Hills

approaching the road at Vale End *(do not cross)* take an immediate right turn on a footpath at TQ0435 4791.

Walk on alongside Waterloo Pond on the right. Join an access lane on a bend, here turn left. Walk on past the delightful Mill Reach private residences. When the lane bends left take the enclosed path on the right at TQ0391 4793 going ahead with a field on the left. This enclosed path emerges into an open area, continue on ahead. Go over a step stile and into a field continue on ahead alongside a ditch on the left. Exit over a step stile and enter another field continue on ahead. Exit over a step stile to meet an unsurfaced lane at TQ0332 4767, here turn left on the Downs Link. In 350m and after passing riding stables at Lockner Farm reach a road *(A248)*.

Cross over the road and go forward up the lane opposite soon passing over a railway bridge. In a further 50m go up the path to the right of a gate at a residence. Exit the path after 750m at a lane by residences. Cross over the lane half-right and enter a National Trust wooded area. Continue on the main path ahead ignoring other paths passing a WWI memorial to the left. The path descends to a T-junction, here turn left and in 40m reach a road *(Sampleoak Lane)*.

For the Villagers public house turn left along the road. In 100m turn left along a track and in 200m reach the Villagers public house.

Cross over the road and continue on the broad track ahead. In 100m at a Y-junction take the left-hand fork. After 400m at a diagonal cross track continue on ahead in the same direction. After 800m at Great Tangley Manor Farm buildings and residences reach an access track on a bend keep on head in the same direction. 100m before the end of the access track meets a road *(B2128)*, turn right on a path through Wonersh Common wooded area. Exit the common at a road *(A2128, Wonersh Common Rd)*.

Cross over the road diagonally right and go down the path to the right of a residence. Continue on this path for about 250m and 30m beyond a Downs Link notice board at a T-junction of tracks continue on ahead on a track *(signed The Tower)* leaving the Downs Link. At a Y-junction bear left and in a few metres cross over a cross track and continue on up the hill. At a T-junction of tracks turn right. In 50m turn left uphill, cross over a cross track and continue on ahead to reach the Tower on Chinthurst Hill at TQ0131 4584. Walk on beyond the tower and begin to go down the hill on the other side bearing right on a path leading amongst the trees. At an inverse Y-junction bear left downhill. Soon meeting an access lane at a U-bend.

Continue in the same direction and follow the lane round to the left and downhill. Pass Chinthurst Hill Lodge and meet a lane, here turn right. At a road junction with Tannery Lane on the left and *"Southlands"* residence on the right turn right along the Downs Link. After 500m where the path turns sharp right leave the Downs Link and go forward over a step stile and continue on ahead. At a T-junction of tracks turn right. Before a farmhouse go over a step stile and follow the enclosed path round to the left of the farmhouse *(Lower Chinthurst Farm)*. Emerge to join its access drive. Turn left along it. Exit through a gate by a disused kissing gate and walk up to a road *(A248)*, here cross over the road and turn left.

Walk 17

In about 300m at Broadstone Brook turn right down its access drive walking left across a small green and to the left of two entrance gates. Go through a kissing gate and walk across a tiny field. Go over a footbridge over a brook and carry on across a small field. Exit over a step stile in a hedgerow to enter a large sports field. Continue across the field in the same direction between playing areas. Exit over a step stile in a fence line and immediately turn right and continue on ahead to reach a railway crossing.

Go through the gate and cross over this active railway line and continue on the lane ahead. Walk on through East Shalford, cross over the Tillingbourne and keep to the lane. 40m past Manor Farm buildings, go through a gap in the hedgerow on the left and before a gate immediately turn right over a step stile and enter a field. Walk on the right-hand edge of the field alongside the lane. Exit the field in the right-hand corner over a step stile and continue on the right-hand edge of another field. Exit in the right-hand corner of the field. Then go over a step stile and enter another field.

For The Seahorse public house walk along its right hand edge for 25m then bear left across the field. Exit the field in the right-hand corner over a step stile and go down shallow steps and continue on an enclosed track. Walk on past Shalford Mill (on the Tillingbourne) and carry on up to a road (the A281) opposite the The Seahorse Inn public house. Return the same way.

Walk along its right-hand edge and in 25m go over a step stile and turn right down steps to regain the lane almost opposite a T-junction.

Go up the lane almost opposite. Beyond residences the lane becomes a track and alongside a road on the left. Later the track meets the road, and in a further 40m bear right on a track. At a cross track go half-left into the North Downs car park.

Walk 18
Wey Navigation, Wey South path (Disused railway), Downs Link, St Martha's Hill, North Downs Way, Pewley Down.

Map:	OS Explorer 145
Start/Finish points:	North Downs car park Pilgrims Way/Echo Pit Rd, Guildford at TQ0036 4839
Distance:	14.5kms (9 miles)
Time:	4 hrs
Transport:	Rail: Guildford 1.6km off route then bus as below. Shalford 1.3kms off route then bus as below
	Bus: Shalford Rd/Pilgrims Way at Shalford Park Guildford
Places of interest:	Wey Navigation, (Optional to St Catherine's Hill and ruins of chapel) Disused railway, (Optional to Chilworth gunpowder mills), St Martha's Hill, Pewley Down
Refreshments:	*The Parrot Inn ph* Broadford Bridge, *The Villagers ph* Blackheath (300m off route), *Percy Arms ph* Chilworth (500m off route)
Local History Notes:	9, 17, 47, 51, 52, 58, 59, 60
Walk description:	Alongside water navigations, along disused railways, churches and excellent views

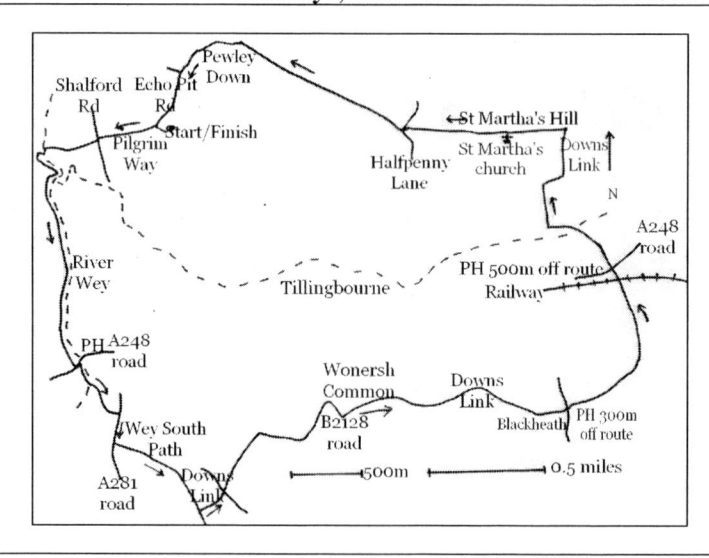

The route

Exit the car park and walk back to the road. At Echo Pit Rd/Pilgrims Way cross over the road and turn left. After 450m exit Pilgrims Way and cross over Shalford Rd. Go forward on the track opposite. Continue on across a field *(Shalford Park)* in the same direction. Once across the field go forward on a track through a tree line and go through a kissing gate then across a plank bridge over a stream and carry on ahead. On reaching the Wey Navigation turn left and soon cross over St Catherine's footbridge to the other bank.

> *Optional detour: Once across St Catherine's footbridge turn left back towards Guildford and in 50m turn left on a track by a small ornamental stone bridge. In a few metres reach the end of a surfaced access lane (Ferry Lane). Go forward over a railway bridge and just before the lane meets the main road turn left on a track leading up the hill. Cross a cross track and make for the highest point on the hill to reach the remains of the chapel of St Catherine and good views – return the same way.*

Having gained the other bank turn right and continue the walk along the Wey Navigation now on the left. At St Catherine's Lock carry on in the same direction. Go underneath a railway bridge and in a further 500m reach a road bridge *(Broadford Bridge)*. Gain the road level and turn left and cross the bridge.

> For the Parrot Inn continue along the right-hand side of the road for 200m.

Immediately turn right and cross over the road and go down the enclosed footpath alongside the Wey Navigation now on the right. Continue on a surfaced path go forward on a surfaced access drive to residences. Exit Stonebridge Wharf at Stonebridge Wharf and Stonebridge Bridge Fields to reach a main road *(A281)*.

Cross over the road and turn right. Opposite Trunley Heath Rd at a T-junction turn left on a broad track joining the Wey South footpath. In 100m cross over the Wey & Arun Junction canal. After 800m pass underneath a road arch bridge at TQ0058 4574. Here turn immediately left and in a few metres at a track junction turn left again joining the Downs Link and go forward to meet a road *(Tannery Lane)*, here turn right.

Walk on past a telephone box and Drodges Close and carry on ahead on a path in front of residences. In 50m go left down a slope to join the road. Here turn right and in 30m at a triangular T-junction go forward on the lane opposite passing Southlands. After 475m at the top of the hill ignore the stile on the left and continue on the path round to the right. At a T-junction of tracks turn left and in 300m reach a road *(B2128)* by a residence.

Cross over the road half-right and enter Wonersh Common woodland. Exit the path at a lane, here turn left. Continue up the lane which becomes unsurfaced to a point where the lane goes left by Great Tangley Manor Farm buildings and residences. Here bear right and cross a cross track, here carry on up a path, which becomes narrower after 50m. After 800m at a diagonal junction of tracks continue on the broad track ahead in the same direction. Maintain this broad track to reach a road *(Sampleoak Lane)*.

> For The Villagers ph turn right along the road. In 100m turn left along a track and in 200m reach The Villagers ph.

Cross over the road and continue on the track ahead. In 40m at a T-junction turn right. Follow the track ahead ignoring others soon passing a WW I memorial on the right. Exit to an access lane by residences. Cross over the lane half-right and go down the enclosed path opposite. Continue down this path which duals with a bridleway before becoming singular. Exit the path to a lane by a residence *(Lockner Lodge)* and go over a railway bridge and walk down to a road *(A248)*.

> For the Percy Arms ph turn left along the road for 500m.

Cross over the road and go down the lane opposite. After 350m cross over the Tillingbourne.

> Optional detour to Chilworth Gunpowder mills: Just over the bridge turn left along a track, return the same way.

Continue on for a further 250m to reach a T-junction of tracks, here turn right and carry on uphill. Continue up St Martha's Hill to reach a cross track *(North Downs Way/Pilgrims Way)* by a WWII pillbox *(at a terminal point of the Downs Link)*. Here turn left on the North Downs Way.

Carry on this broad sandy track ignoring others and reach St Martha's church at St Martha's Hill. Enter the churchyard through a gate *(notice the commemorative stone to Yvonne Arnaud on the left)* and walk up to the church. *(Near the church entrance notice the grave of Gen Freyberg VC.)* Continue through the churchyard and exit through a gate and proceed on the broad sandy North Downs Way track leading downhill. After 700m reach an access drive to a residence by a car park. Cross over the drive and continue on the track ahead to reach a lane at Southernway Cottage.

Pewley Down

Photo L Ham

Here turn left and in about 25m turn right on a broad track. In a further 10m at a Y-junction take the right fork. In less than 100m at a junction of tracks bear right. Later the track duals by a low fence then becomes singular

Walk 18

before reaching a cross track. Cross over the track half-left to enter Pewley Down. Continue on the long enclosed track ahead. After passing through a hedgerow at a Y-junction bear left and in 15m at a second Y-junction bear right leading uphill. At the top of the hill bear left. Carry on to reach a marker stone at TQ0075 4897.

Proceed on in the same direction and at the end of a tree line turn left downhill. Cross over a cross track and continue on downhill. Exit the track at an access drive to residences. Carry on down the drive *(Northdown Lane)* to reach a junction of roads. Continue on in the same direction down Echo Pit Rd. After 270m bear left on a broad track and in a further 150m reach the North Downs car park.

Walk 19
Tilling Spring, Wotton, Abinger Hammer, Gomshall, Shere, Albury, Waterloo Pond, Chilworth, East Shalford, Shalford

Map:	OS Explorer 146 and 145
Start point:	Tilling Spring at TQ1400 4487
Finish point:	River Wey Navigation at SU9951 4804
Distance:	22.5kms (14 miles)
Time:	5½ hrs
Transport:	Rail: Gomshall, Chilworth, Shalford, Guildford
Bus:	Wotton Hatch, Abinger Hammer, Gomshall, Shere, Albury, Chilworth, Shalford
Places of interest:	Tilling Spring, Waterfall, Wotton, Abinger Hammer, Gomshall, Shere, Albury, Waterloo Pond, East Shalford, Shalford, and the River Wey Navigation
Refreshments:	*Wotton Hatch ph* Wotton, *The Abinger Arms ph* Abinger Hammer, Gomshall Mill, *The Black Horse ph The Compasses ph* and shops Gomshall, *The White Horse ph, The Prince of Wales ph,* Shops and Tea shops Shere, *Drummond Arms ph* Albury, *The Seahorse Inn ph* Shalford
Local History Notes:	2, 5, 6, 29, 47, 48, 49, 55, 58, 61
Walk description:	A 14 mile walk following the course of the Tillingbourne from its spring in the Surrey hills to its outlet into the River Wey Navigation. Passing through the delightful Surrey hills and villages. Some road/lane walking

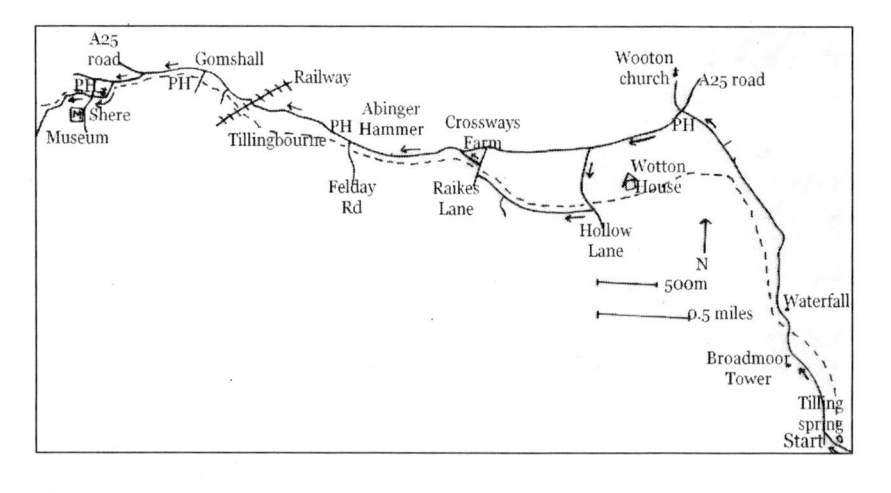

Walk 19

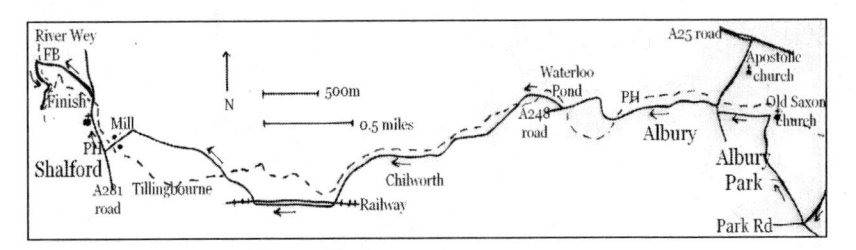

Positioning options
The Tillingbourne begins its course from the north side of Leith Hill and as such it is remote from public transport or car parks. Therefore a positioning walk is required to locate to the start of the walk. There are three likely options, first, is to walk from Wotton Hatch to the source, which will mean that the first part of the walk proper is a duplication of this positioning walk in reverse. The second option is to begin the walk from Coldharbour village, which would probably mean taking alternative transport to Coldharbour. The third option is to get a friend to drop you off at Pond cottage and walk on to the Tilling Spring.

The first option:
Leaving Wotton Hatch public house on the A25 walk away from the A25 along Damphurst Lane. After 200m and opposite Wotton Hatch cottages turn left along an access drive for 5m and take the enclosed path on the right which runs parallel to the lane. Exit the path to reach a lane at a cottage. Here join the Greensand Way, walk forward along the access drive to the cottage and continue on the track. After 1 km at a track junction bear right on the broad track and pass by a pond on the right. At a Y-junction keep to the right fork. The path eventually meets a lane walk along it for 15m and then turn left on a broad track. Maintain the track and direction ignoring others. Pass by Pond cottage and continue on ahead. At a Y-junction of tracks at TQ1390 4500 bear left leaving the Greensand Way and in 200m reach the general area of the Tilling Spring at TQ1400 4487.

The Second Option:
Facing The Plough Inn, Coldharbour walk right in a southerly direction passing a telephone box on the left soon walking alongside a row of residences on a broad track. At a Y-junction take the right fork (signed the Tower). In 100m turn right on a narrow track leading steeply uphill. At a faint cross track continue on uphill. At a second faint cross track continue on uphill. At a Y-junction bear right and walk over the top of the hill maintaining direction ignoring other tracks. Then descend to a track junction by a centrally positioned tree. Cross over the broad cross track at this junction and continue on the track opposite downhill. Cross over a cross track and in 25m reach a T-junction at a broad track. Here turn right and in 5m bear left to a multi track junction at TQ1457 4433. Walk left through an earth banking and immediately take the broad track on the right on bearing 320 degrees leading downhill ignoring the lesser track to its right. At a broad Y-junction maintain direction on the right fork which exits Duke's Warren to join an access track to residences. Continue on ahead in the same direction. In less than 200m reach the start point at Tilling Spring at TQ1400 4487.

84   The Surrey Hills

> **The Third Option:** Get a friend to drop you off at Pond cottage. From the Wotton Hatch on the (A25) drive along Sheephouse Lane. Turn left to Broadmoor village. Turn left along the unsurfaced single track Greensand Way for 500m as far as Pond cottage. Walk on as in option one.

The route

Facing the pond at the Tilling Spring at TQ1400 4487 walk left and slightly downhill on a broad track. At a junction of tracks bear right joining the Greensand Way. Later pass by Pond Cottage and continue on ahead.

Pond at the source of the Tillingbourne
Photo L Ham

Maintain direction ignoring other tracks for a further 500m to reach a lane at TQ1356 4569 at Broadmoor village.

Here turn right and in 10m bear right on a broad track. Later cross over the Tillingbourne and in a further 120m pass by a waterfall on the right.

> *Optional Detour:* At various points along this path it is possible to cross over step stiles on the left to get closer views of the Tillingbourne. Return to the main path same way.

At a Y-junction of tracks bear left maintaining the broad track. The path eventually exits at an access drive to a cottage and then meets a lane.

Walk 19

Cross over the track to the right of the lane and go through a tree line. Immediately at the corner of a field take the left enclosed track parallel to the lane so continuing in much the same direction. Exit the path where an access drive joins the lane *(Damphurst Lane)*.

Gain the lane and turn right along it. Exit the lane at a junction with the A25 road by the *Wotton Hatch* public house.

Cross over the road and turn left along the footpath along the A25. After 850m at a road T-junction on the left, turn left along Hollow Lane. After 450m and just past a residence on the left cross over the Tillingbourne and in a further 150m turn sharp right over a step stile by a gate and go forward on the broad track into Townhurst Wood.

Optional Detour: At one or two places along this path it is possible to detour on paths to the right to gain sight of the Tillingbourne, return the same way.

In about 750m the track draws very close to the Tillingbourne, maintain the path ahead, which becomes enclosed and leads up to a wide gate and a step stile. Go over the step stile and gain a lane *(Abinger Lane)* on a bend.

Continue on in the same direction along the lane and in 60m pass the entrance to Abinger Mill which is now a private residence. Exit Abinger Lane at a small triangular junction and turn right along Raikes Lane.

Cross over the Tillingbourne and in 10m turn left over a step stile to enter a field. Go forward on the track ahead *(on the right is Crossways Farm)*.

Optional Detour: In a few metres it is possible to follow a track to the left alongside the Tillingbourne, the track effectively ends at a makeshift footbridge. Here at the "No Entry" sign it is advisable to turn back as the path soon peters out. Return the same way.

Continue across the field in the same direction as from the step stile. Exit over a step stile to gain the A25 road.

Tillingbourne at Abinger Hammer   Photo L Ham

The Surrey Hills

Cross over the road and turn left and walk along the footpath. The footpath finally descends to regain the road *(A25)* opposite an access drive to Paddington Farm, here cross over the road.

Optional detour: Walk down the access drive for a sight of a fishing pond created by the Tillingbourne, backtrack to the A25.

Carry on along the A25 on a footpath towards Abinger Hammer now on its left-hand side. The stone wall on the left conceals the Tillingbourne just over the other side. At a T-junction with Felday Rd opposite the post office cross over Felday Rd and turn left down it. Cross over the Tillingbourne and immediately turn right over a plank bridge. Go forward and walk alongside the Tillingbourne on the edge of a sports field. In 150m turn right over a footbridge over the Tillingbourne and walk up to the road (A25), here turn left.

Walk on through Abinger Hammer passing the hammer bell and clock tower and *Abinger Arms* public house on the right. About 200m beyond the village turn left on a broad unsurfaced access drive. Continue on past residences then cross over the Tillingbourne. Before the entrance to Brook Cottage take the right of two tracks leading uphill to the left of the entrance. At an inverse Y-junction continue on in the same direction. At a T-junction of tracks at Southbrooks Farm turn right on a broad track. *(The Tillingbourne can be seen across the field to the right.)* Maintain the broad track ignoring others, cross over the Tillingbourne and go forward towards the A25. Before meeting the A25 proper turn left through a foot tunnel underneath the railway. Exit to meet the A25, turn left along it.

Jack the Hammer   Abinger Hammer
                                        Photo's L Ham

Walk 19

At Gomshall Mill observe the Tillingbourne and again on the left by the *Compasses Inn*. Continue along the A25 through Gomshall.

> *Optional Detour: At Queen St, on the left, turn left for 10m to view the Tillingbourne, return back to the A25.*

Continue on the A25, immediately past Queen St pass by The King John House on the left and later pass by The Old Netley Mill. At a T-junction with Gomshall Lane bear left maintaining the footpath along Gomshall Lane.

On approaching Shere and 20m past Tillingbourne cottage, on the left, turn left on a footpath. Cross over a footbridge over the Tillingbourne and enter the churchyard of St James. Turn right and walk past the church *(notice the plaque on the north wall of the church dedicated to the Anchoress of Shere)*. Exit the churchyard through a lych-gate and walk to the centre of the village opposite the *White Horse* public house in Shere.

Cross over the road and turn right to gain the Tillingbourne at a bridge at Middle St/Lower St. Walk alongside the Tillingbourne along Lower St. At the ford continue on the broad track ahead. Turn right through a kissing gate and walk alongside the Tillingbourne. Exit through a kissing gate *(Vicky's Gate)*.

Turn left and in 15m turn right through a kissing gate and go forward uphill on a broad grassy track in Albury Estate. Exit through a kissing gate to reach a road *(Park Rd)*.

Gomshall Mill over the Tillingbourne   Photo L Ham

Here turn very sharp right through a metal gate to re-enter Albury Estate and Albury Park. Walk on past the Lodge and in about 150m go left and right then maintain direction. At a cross track continue on in the same direction. The track begins to descend and towards the bottom at a Y-junction take the right-hand fork. Soon exit through a kissing gate and go forward down to reach an access drive.

Bear right across the grass to view the Old Saxon church. At the churchyard gate do an about turn and walk east either along the access drive or alongside the Tillingbourne to its right. Exit Albury Estate through a gate by a Lodge at New Rd.

Here turn right and in 25m meet a road *(A248)* on a bend at TQ0576 4790.

Further along the A248 to the right is the Tillingbourne and the Apostolic Church.

At this road junction turn left *(signed Albury, Chilworth)* and walk along an elevated path alongside the road. The path descends to road level; continue on the footpath through Albury passing fishponds and the *Drummond Arms* public house. 100m beyond the post office and Church Lane cross over the Tillingbourne and continue on the footpath on the A248 passing Weston Farm, on the left. Continue past the end of Water Lane and Guildford Lane, on the right. Carry on along Chilworth Lane. At Vale End fisheries, on the left, cross over the road and take the enclosed footpath to the left of the access drive to Vale End at TQ0435 4791.

Walk on alongside Waterloo Pond on the right. Join an access lane on a bend, here turn left. Walk on past the delightful Mill Reach private residences and Postford pond. When the lane bends left take the enclosed path on the right at TQ0391 4793 going ahead with a field on the left. This enclosed path emerges into an open area, continue on ahead. Go over a step stile and into a field continue on ahead alongside a ditch on the left. Exit over a step stile and enter another field continue on ahead. Exit over a step stile to meet an unsurfaced lane at TQ0332 4767.

Here turn right and cross over the Tillingbourne and immediately turn left on a path. Walk on for 900m keeping to the main path and passing the remains of Chilworth Gunpowder Mills (1625-1920) with evidence of the Tillingbourne on both sides of the path. Exit through a metal gate by a lodge to reach a lane *(Blacksmiths Lane). (A bridge over the Tillingbourne is to the right and beyond are picturesque fishponds.)*

Cross over the lane and continue on the surfaced access drive opposite to a commercial area. Immediately past Rose Cottage, on the right, bear right into a sunken channel and go forward on an enclosed track behind commercial buildings. Exit through a gate and go forward on a footpath across a private garden area, exiting through a gate. Go forward and bear left before Meadow cottage. Cross an open area and later enter a wooded area. Go through a metal kissing gate and go forward up steps to cross an active railway line. Continue on the path behind residences, go through a metal kissing gate and carry on ahead. Maintain the path ignoring others and exit at a lane by a railway crossing.

Here turn right and cross the active railway line. Walk on through East Shalford village soon crossing over the Tillingbourne. Keep to the lane and 40m past Manor Farm buildings *(on the right)* go through a gap in the hedgerow on the left and before a gate immediately turn right over a step stile. Walk on the right-hand edge of the field. Exit the field in the right-hand corner over a step stile and continue on the right-hand edge of another field. Exit in the right-hand corner of the field. Then go over a step stile and enter another field. Walk along its right-hand edge and in 25m by a step stile *(do not cross)* turn left and walk across the field. Exit the field in the right-hand corner over a step stile and go down shallow steps and continue on an enclosed track. Walk on past Shalford Mill *(on the Tillingbourne)* and carry on up to a road *(the A281)* opposite the *The Seahorse Inn* public house. Here turn right.

Optional Detour: In 150m at East Shalford Lane you may turn right and walk down the lane for 40m to Lemon Bridge to view the Tillingbourne. Retrace your steps back to the A281 and continue on along it.

Along the road is No 34 The Street. Across from the church and behind a high brick wall is the house called Debnershe, see notes.

Cross over the road and maintain the A281 past St Mary the Virgin church. Cross over a footbridge over the Tillingbourne. Continue along the A281 and immediately past Bridge House take the footpath on the left to gain Shalford Park. Bear left and join a surfaced footpath.

Optional Detour: In the left-hand corner you may bear left and walk for a few metres to a bridge over the Tillingbourne. At this point you are about 200m from the outlet of the Tillingbourne, here do an about turn and walk back into the park.

On returning from the detour, turn left and follow the tree line for 400m and then turn left on a track through the trees. Go through a kissing gate and cross over a stream and continue on up to the River Wey Navigation. At the river turn left and in a few metres turn right over a footbridge to gain the other bank. At the bottom of the steps turn right along the other bank passing sand landslides. Walk on round a sharp right-hand bend in the river and in a further 100m at SU9951 4804, on the opposite bank, is where the flow from the Tillingbourne joins the River Wey proper and the end of the walk.

Walk 20 The Roof of Surrey

Box Hill, Brockham Hill, Deepdene, The Glory Wood, The Nower, Coldharbour (Anstiebury fort), Leith Hill, Somerset Hill, Holmbury Hill, Pitch Hill, Reynards Hill, Winterfold Hill, Barnett Hill, Chinthurst Hill, Pewley Down, St Martha's Hill, Newlands Corner, Hackhurst Downs, Ranmore Common, Stepping Stones, Box Hill.

Map:	OS Explorer 146 and 145
Start/Finish points:	Box Hill observation platform TQ1797 5118
Distance:	69.2 kms (44 miles)
Time:	17¾ hr
Transport:	Rail: Box Hill and Westhumble, Dorking, Deepdene, Gomshall (off route), Shalford (off route), Guildford (Off route). Bus: Box Hill, Brockham, Dorking, Westcott, Coldharbour, Holmbury St Mary (Pitland Street), Peaslake, Wonersh, Shalford, Guildford (off route), Shere (off route), Ranmore, Westhumble (A24) *Some of these locations are served infrequently*
Places of interest:	Burford Bridge Hotel, Labelliere headstone, Swiss Cottage, Box Hill fort, Box Hill, Brockham, Deepdene, The Glory Wood, The Temple, Coldharbour, Anstiebury fort, Leith Hill, Leith Hill Tower, Holmbury Hill fort, Duke of Kent School, Pitch Hill, Ewhurst windmill, Summerfold House, Raynards Hill, Winterfold Hill, Barnett Hill, Wonersh, Chinthurst Hill, East Shalford, Pewley Down, St Martha's Hill, St Martha's church, Newlands Corner, Ranmore, Denbies, Burford Corner River Mole and the Stepping Stones
Refreshments:	The car park by Ryka's Cafe, Box Hill, Brockham, Dorking, Coldharbour, Leith Hill (restricted), Pitland Street, Pitch Hill (off route), Wonersh, Shalford (off route), Newlands Corner, Shere (off route), Westhumble (off route)
Local History Notes:	10, 12, 18, 19, 20, 21, 22, 23, 31, 32, 34, 38, 41, 43, 44, 46, 48, 52, 60
Walk description:	A magnificent circular hilltop walk with glorious views, villages, woods and forests walking on either side of the Tillingbourne valley on the chalk to the north and greensand to the south. It can be walked in sections.

Walk 20

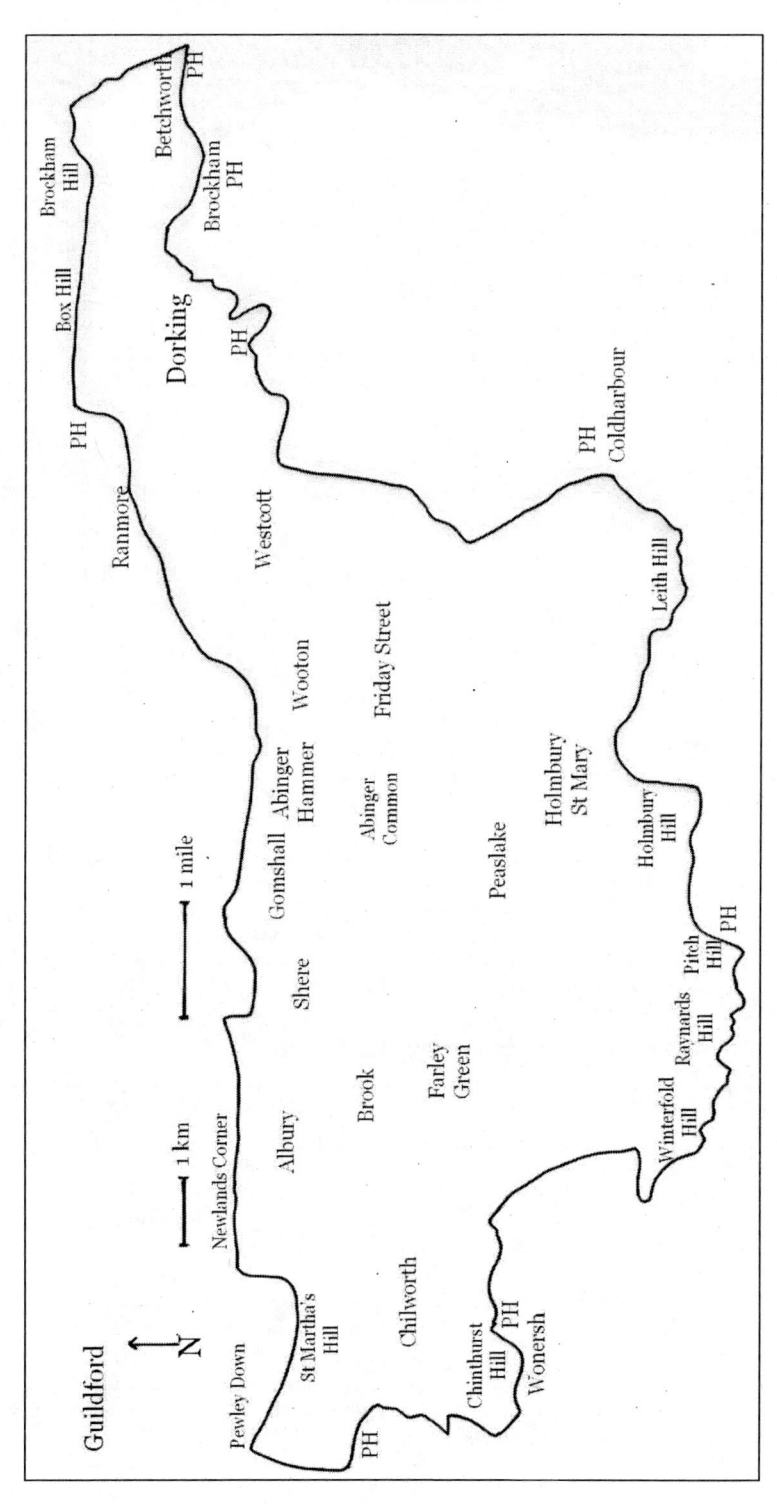

The route
Section 1
Box Hill to Brockham 6.5kms (4 miles) 1½ hrs

Note: The start and finish points to this walk is the Box Hill observation platform at TQ1797 5118. To reach that point from the nearest car park, bus stop or Box Hill and Westhumble railway station follow the route description below using a start point for this as the car park by Ryka's Cafe at TQ1719 5202.

Exit the car park by Ryka's Cafe (at TQ1719 5202) and cross over the road (Old London Rd) towards Box Hill. Go through a gap in the fence and turn right and walk up a steep stepped track to ascend the side of Box Hill. The steps give way to a steep chalky track. Keep to the left of a tree line and walk round its left-hand edge and carry on up the hill. Later bear right to follow a broad chalk track ignoring others. Where the track narrows go forward to pass the Labelliere headstone.

Continue on and in 80m where the path begins to go downhill at a T-junction, turn left by a centrally located tree trunk. Carry on and soon reach Swiss Cottage on the right. Continue on the path ahead to reach a road, here turn right.

The path then veers away from the road and goes down to an observation and trig point on Box Hill at TQ1797 5118.

Facing the view and leaving the observation platform on Box Hill at TQ1797 5118 walk left *(east)* away from the observation point along the North Downs Way. After 100m at a Y-junction bear left. Maintain this path ignoring others. Go through a gate and later go through a second gate and carry on ahead. Maintain direction ignoring other tracks. In a wooded area the path dips down and up steps twice before continuing slowly downhill through the woodland. Later the path swings sharp left up steps. At the top of the steps turn right. At an inverse Y-junction go forward down steps. At the bottom of the steps at a T-junction of tracks turn left. At a Y-junction at TQ1956 5133, by a notice board, bear right.

Just before some steps, look to the left, and notice the grave of "Quick" An English Thoroughbred 1936-1944.

Carry on down the steps to a T-junction of tracks, here turn right downhill. Continue on downhill to reach a T-junction of tracks by a notice board at TQ2035 5136, here turn right leaving the North Downs Way.

The track later goes left *(hard to spot)* and then over a cross track *(Pilgrims' Way)*. Continue forward and go over a step stile and enter a field. Carry on ahead across the field on a faint track on bearing about 140 degrees. Cross over a bridge over the railway and go over a step stile and enter another field. Walk half left for 50m then turn right to walk along the left-hand side of a tree line. Cross over a step stile and reach the A25 road.

Walk 20

Staines Ramblers at Box Hill   Photo L Ham

Cross this very busy road and go over a step stile and enter a small field. Cross the field slightly left on a faint track. Exit in the left-hand corner of the field through a gap to enter another field. Continue on ahead alongside a right fence. Follow the path round the edge of the field which later goes left and becomes enclosed eventually going left again on another enclosed path between residences. The track emerges at a road by a post office.

Cross over the road and turn left and in 30m turn right by a bus stop on a surfaced path. Eventually the path meets a road, continue on along it in the same direction. At a T-junction *(on the left)* by the *Dolphin Inn ph*, Betchworth, turn right up a surfaced track on the Greensand Way.

Village well and Green, Brockham Photo L Ham

Enter the churchyard through an arched doorway of St Michael's church Betchworth. Walk on through the churchyard exiting through a gate. Cross over an access lane and continue on the track ahead. Go through a gate and enter a large field, continue on its left-hand edge *(later note the WWII pillbox on the left)*. Exit through a gate and carry on ahead. Cross a footbridge over a ditch. At a T-junction with a broad track turn left ignoring the path on the right. At a Y-junction go left over a footbridge over the River Mole and continue on a narrow surfaced track. Cross over a bridge and go through a gate at the terminal point of an access lane in Brockham.

Here turn right and walk on past the *Dukes Head* and the *Royal Oak* public houses and arrive at the village Green, Brockham.

Section 2
Brockham to Horsham Rd, Dorking 5.2kms (3¼ miles) 1½ hrs

Walk across the village Green and cross over the road passing by the village well and go down Old School Lane. Just after a bridge and where the lane goes left, bear right up a broad unsurfaced track. In 400m where the Greensand Way goes left, continue on ahead past Betchworth Park Golf Course. Eventually the path merges with the access drive to the golf course club house. Immediately past the access drive turn left on a path. Beyond the car park ignore a path on the left and continue on up to Y-junction of tracks, here take the right fork. Maintain this track to a point where it joins a narrow surfaced lane. Continue on ahead in the same direction soon reaching a road *(Punchbowl Lane)*, here turn left.

In about 200m turn sharp right on a road *(Deepdene Wood)*, here rejoining the Greensand Way. At the first T-junction on the left *(signed to Nos 5-29)*, turn left along it. Almost at the end of the road *(Deepdene End)* turn right on a grassy track. Where the track begins to go downhill at a Y-junction at TQ1742 4893, take the right fork down hard to spot steps downhill through rhododendron bushes. At the bottom of the hill, at a cross track turn right. Continue on down to the A24 road at TQ1720 4897.

Cross over this very busy road and turn left. Pass the end of Chart Lane and in a few metres bear right into The Glory Wood. At a Y-junction take the right fork. At a T-junction of tracks turn right. At a junction of tracks bear right and go through a gate. Exit the wood to an open area and in 20m at a Y-junction before a seat bear right downhill. Exit The Glory Wood proper through a gate and continue on the unsurfaced access road ahead. At a T-junction turn left along St Pauls Rd West.

Where it meets a road on a bend continue on ahead in the same direction. In about 150m turn right along Peacock Walk. In just over 100m turn left on a narrower enclosed surfaced footpath. Exit the path by the *Queen's Head* public house on Horsham Rd, Dorking.

Section 3
Horsham Rd, Dorking to Leith Hill 9kms (6 miles) 2½ hrs

Cross over the end of Horsham Rd and turn right for a few metres to the junction. Turn left along South St and walk up to a T-junction with Falkland Rd/Vincent Lane. Cross over the end of Falkland Rd and turn right and in a few metres turn left up a surfaced enclosed walkway.

At the top of the walkway meet the terminal point of a road *(Nower Rd)*, here continue on ahead. At a T-junction of roads turn left and walk to its terminal point at a T-junction with Hamstead Lane.

Here turn right and in 20m cross over the road and bear left to walk past a wide gate. Go forward alongside a tall hedgerow. At the point of the hedgerow and on entering a large open grassy area turn left still following the hedgerow. At the end of the tree line and at a junction of tracks by an entrance gate *(on the left)* continue on the track uphill. At the top of the hill in just over a 100m at a Y-junction bear right and walk over The Nower. Maintain this track with glimpses of views to left and right for 700m to reach the Temple at TQ1555 4844. Continue on past the Temple soon passing a wooden barrier and continue on a steep downhill track. At the bottom of the hill at a junction of tracks bear left soon reaching a surfaced access drive, here turn left.

Where the lane goes left before a residence bear right down an access track and in 10m the Greensand Way goes off to the right, take the left fork soon going underneath a wooden footbridge. The track emerges at an access lane at TQ1499 4840 here turn left.

At the terminal point of the lane walk on past residences and go through a metal kissing gate by a gate continuing on the track ahead. Ignore the footbridge on the right and the bridge and cross over a lane and continue on the track ahead. Cross over a broad track and continue on ahead. Where a path comes in from the left by a gate, go forward over a fence stile and enter a field. Walk along its right-hand edge. Exit in the top right-hand corner of the field over a step stile and go forward on a track between tree lines. Go over a log bridge that supports a step stile over a ditch and enter a field. Continue up the left-hand edge. Exit the field almost in the left-hand corner over a step stile by a gate to gain a lane at TQ1484 4678.

Cross over the lane and continue on the track opposite *(signed Squire Farm)*. Walk between and past the farm buildings and farmhouse and continue on an enclosed track that goes round to the left. Then enter a wooded area. After about 300m at a Y-junction at TQ1429 4613 take the left fork. At a broad cross track on a bend at TQ1447 4556 cross over the track and continue on the uphill track opposite. At a T-junction by a residence at TQ1445 4521 turn left on a broad track *(Wolvens Lane)*.

At a 5 track junction at TQ1488 4469 continue on the broad track in the same direction on bearing about 140 degrees. Maintain this broad track ignoring all others eventually emerging to a surfaced lane in Coldharbour. At a T-junction at TQ1511 4410 reach the village of Coldharbour opposite *The Plough Inn* public house.

> *Optional detour to Anstiebury Hill fort site: Facing The Plough Inn public house in Coldharbour walk left along the lane. After about 300m at a lane junction turn right and in about 100m reach an entrance area to the fort on the right. Return to Coldharbour village the same way.*

Coldharbour village · Photo L Ham

Here turn right and walk in a southerly direction passing a telephone box on the left soon walking alongside a row of residences on a broad track. At a Y-junction take the right fork *(signed the Tower)*. Later pass Coldharbour cricket field on the right. After the cricket field, at a Y-junction, take the left fork. Maintain this broad obvious track ignoring others. When the track starts to go downhill meet a four track junction. Here turn right and in 10m take the right-hand fork downhill. The track descends to another multi track junction where it meets the Greensand Way, here turn left uphill along the Greensand Way *(signed Leith Hill Tower)*. Continue up this broad stony track to arrive at the Tower on Leith Hill at TQ1396 4316.

Section 4
Leith Hill to Winterfold Hill 12.5kms 7¾ miles 3 hrs

From Leith Hill Tower walk in a westerly direction maintaining the Greensand Way on a broad track downhill *(signed Starveall Corner car park)*. Just after where the track narrows, bear left on a track *(signed to car park)*. Re-cross the broad track diagonally right and maintain the "*footpath to car park*". Re-join the broad track and soon meet a broad cross track. Cross over the track diagonally right walking to the left of the car park icon. Descend to a road *(Leith Hill Rd)* at TQ1309 4318. Cross over the road diagonally right and walk through a lay-by car park at Starveall Corner.

Continue on the track ahead. Ignore a farm cross track and in a further 100m at a junction of tracks turn right. Continue on this track for 350m ignoring others to reach a left T-junction at TQ1285 4354, here turn left on a farm access track *(signed to High Ashes Farm)*. Just before the entrance to the farm bear left on a track. Maintain this track for 1.5kms *(nearly 1 mile)*. Exit at a lane *(Pasturewood Rd)*, here turn left. Exit Pasturewood Rd at a T-junction.

Here turn right and in 40m turn left into Pitland Street *(notice the plaque on the corner cottage)*. Continue up the hill through the village and along Holmbury Hill Rd. In 40m, turn very sharp right up a broad track. At the top of the track at an inverse Y-junction at TQ1094 4340 bear left on a broad track. Eventually after 650m reach a multi track junction at Somerset Hill at TQ1057 4361, here turn left.

At a Y-junction bear right maintaining the Greensand Way. Contour round Holmbury Hill then follow the path up to the Holmbury Hill view point at TQ1041 4293. Leave Holmbury Hill along the Greensand Way, to the left of a concrete donations box. Maintain the Greensand Way ignoring all other tracks. Cross over an open area and continue on the path opposite. Enter Holmbury Hill car park and turn left. Walk down its access drive to reach a road *(Radnor Rd)*.

Cross over the road and take the left fork of two paths going downhill to soon join another path, continue on downhill. At a junction of paths turn right. Then walk across a valley on an enclosed track passing through *The McKinney Gate*. Go over a hill and continue on another enclosed track between fields across another valley. Later behind residences cross over a step stile and carry on ahead. The path descends to a road opposite the entrance to the Duke of Kent School.

Cross over the road and walk along the surfaced access drive into the school grounds. In about 130m take the path to the right of the road. Then continue up shallow steps and carry on the track uphill veering left to exit through a kissing gate leaving the school grounds. Continue on the uphill track.

All weather walkers in the Surrey Hills
Photo L Ham

Ascend steps and cross over a cross track and ascend more steps and carry on ahead. The track emerges at a broad track at TQ0864 4287, here turn left. At the end of a surfaced access drive continue on ahead. In a further 100m turn right on a track leading uphill. The track meets a broad track at a T-junction, here turn left. At a Y-junction bear left and continue on up to the viewpoint at Pitch Hill at TQ0830 4227, where it is possible to see the sea.

Holmbury Hill   Photo L Ham

Walk away from the viewpoint and bear left up to the trig point. Continue on past the trig point and a concrete donations box and continue on a broad track, the Greensand Way on bearing about 320 degrees. The path descends to a car park. Exit the car park through its access gate.

For the Windmill (Bar/restaurant) turn left down the road for 300m.

Cross over the road and walk up the access drive past Windmill house ignoring the track on the right. Just by the gate to Mill cottage turn right up a track. The track emerges at an access track by Four Winds residence and Ewhurst Windmill, continue on to a Y-junction, here take the left fork. In a further 100m where the track goes left to a residence continue on ahead in the same direction on a narrower track. Cross over two unsurfaced access drives, to Summerfold House, and carry on down to a road T-junction.

Go forward along the road opposite then turn left through a small car park and continue on the Greensand Way uphill. *(Soon reaching viewpoints of the Weald and the South Downs at Reynards Hill at TQ1040 4293.)* Continue on in the same direction along the Greensand Way. At a Y-junction bear right and in 30m at a second Y-junction keep to the right fork. Maintain direction parallel to a lane *(on the right)* eventually joining it in a dip, here turn left and walk along the lane. In 70m turn left on a track soon going up shallow steps, carry on ahead. Maintain the twisting track through woodland crossing over a surfaced narrow lane. At a T-junction of tracks turn right. Maintain this track and direction ignoring other tracks. Reach Winterfold Hill at TQ0630 4270.

Section 5
Winterfold Hill to Wonersh 9kms (6 miles) 2½ hrs

Continue on the Greensand Way and walk through the car park No 5 at Winterfold Hill. Maintain the obvious track ignoring all others. At a second car park at TQ0587 4271 turn left after 25m on a track soon going down steps to meet a lane. Cross over the lane and carry on the track opposite. After about 250m at a Y-junction leave the Greensand Way and take the right fork. At a second Y-junction take the right fork. Cross over a cross track by a gate and carry on ahead. Go through a gate and join the end of an access lane at residences *(Madgehole Farm).*

Walk 20

Here turn left and walk down the access lane passing Madgehole Farm. After 700m where the lane goes sharp left at residences, turn right on a broad track *(Madgehole Lane)*. Continue up this track for 850m and turn left on a wide track at TQ0559 4363. In 50m turn left at a left T-junction. Maintain this uphill track ignoring others. At the top reach a Y-junction of tracks at TQ0541 4396, here continue on in the same direction on bearing about 10 degrees on a sandy track. At an inverse Y-junction continue on ahead and in a further 30m at a junction of tracks continue on in much the same direction on bearing about 340 degrees. In a further 150m meet a broad unsurfaced access track at TQ0533 4428, here turn left. In a further 450m reach a lane *(Farley Heath Rd)*.

Cross over the lane and go forward 20m and pass by a wide gate and join a broad track at a T-junction, here turn right. Maintain this bridle track which later narrows. At a junction of wide tracks continue on in the same direction on bearing about 350 degrees. Maintain this track ignoring all others. The track emerges from woodland at a T-junction with a broad track underneath telephone lines, here turn left. In 50m reach a triangular junction of lanes by a residence, here bear right along a surfaced access lane. At the terminal point of the lane where it goes left into residences continue on ahead on a track into woodland. Maintain this broad track for 400m, ignoring others, to reach a cross track at TQ0413 4592, here turn left on bearing about 210 degrees emerging to a heath land *(on the right)*. In just over 100m at a Y-junction take the left fork and walk on across the heath land. The path then descends into woodland. Continue on this broad track ignoring all others. Eventually reaching a car park at TQ0346 4572 at Littleford Lane.

Walk on through the car park and exit at the road. Cross over the road and continue on the footpath opposite on bearing about 290 degrees on a sandy track leading slightly uphill. In about 200m at the corner point of a fence line at TQ0326 4574 turn left passing an open space on the right. Soon the track goes downhill and reaches a junction of tracks at TQ0312 4566, here bear left downhill. In a dip, pass by a cottage and continue on ahead. Later pass by a cemetery on the left, cross over a cross track and continue on the track opposite alongside a fence on the left. At an inverse Y-junction at a broad track turn left uphill. At the top of the hill *(Barnett Hill)* continue on past two wide gates on a broad track. Maintain this track downhill ignoring others. Exit the track and proceed along an unsurfaced drive to reach a road.

Cross over the road and turn right. And in 30m veer left across a grassy area to reach a surfaced footpath by a play area, here turn left and skirt the edge of a sports field. Exit the sports field at Lawnsmead at a road T-junction in Wonersh.

Chinthurst Hill Tower   Photo L Ham

Section 6
Wonersh to St Martha's Hill 8.8kms (5½ miles) 2¼ hrs

Cross over the road and turn left and in 20m turn right up a broad surfaced access drive *(signed to Wonersh Memorial Hall)*. At its terminal point go forward on a grassy area and go forward through a gap in a metal fence line and join a cross track, here turn left. Exit through a metal kissing gate to reach a road *(B2128)*, here turn right. Where the road swings left continue on along a lane *(Chinthurst Lane)* for about 300m where bear right on an access drive at Chinthurst Hill.

Walk on past Chinthurst Hill Lodge. Continue on this access drive later signed private drive. Having almost walked round a right U-bend, ignore the main path to the left by a gate and notice board and continue on a path to the right of the notice board up steps. At a Y-junction take the right fork. On emerging from the tree cover bear round to the left to reach the tower on top of Chinthurst Hill at TQ0131 4584.

With your back to the tower and facing the open view walk to the left on bearing about 20 degrees soon going downhill on a narrow track. Ignore a cross track and continue downhill. Go down a few steps and reach a grassy cross track by a seat. Here turn right and in 50m turn left down steps by another seat. Maintain the general direction downhill to go forward on a track which later meets the Downs Link footpath on a bend. Here turn left and in 375m where the path turns sharp left, go over a step stile on the right leaving the Downs Link. At a T-junction of tracks by a disused step stile turn right. By a farmhouse *(Lower Chinthurst Farm)* go over a step stile and follow the enclosed path round to the left of the farmhouse. Emerge to join the farms access drive. Turn left along it. Exit through a gate by a disused kissing gate and walk up to a road (A248).

Here cross over the road and turn left. In about 300m at Broadstone Brook turn right down its access drive bearing left across a green. Walk to the left of two entrance gates and go through a kissing gate and walk across a tiny field. Go over a footbridge over a brook and walk on across a small field. Exit over a step stile in a hedgerow to enter a large sports field. Walk on across the field due north and between playing areas. Exit over a step stile in a fence line and immediately turn right. At an inverse Y-junction walk on 40m to reach a lane at a railway crossing.

Here turn left and go through the gate and cross over the active railway line and continue on the lane ahead. Walk on through East Shalford village soon crossing over the Tillingbourne. Keep to the lane and 40m past Manor Farm buildings *(on the right)* go through a gap in the hedgerow on the left and before a gate immediately turn right over a step stile. Walk on the right-hand edge of the field alongside the lane. Exit the field in the right-hand corner over a step stile and continue on the right-hand edge of another field. Exit in the right-hand corner of the field over a step stile. Then go over a second step stile and enter another field. Walk along its right-hand edge and in 25m go over a step stile and turn right down steps to regain the lane opposite a T-junction.

Go up the lane opposite. Beyond residences the lane becomes a track and goes alongside a road on the left. Later the track meets the road at a junction of tracks coming in from the right. In a further 40m bear right on a track. At a cross track continue on past the North Downs car park at Chantry Wood at TQ0036 4839 and soon reach a road *(Echo Pit Rd)*.

Here turn right along it. Walk on passing Chantry View Rd. Where the road goes sharp left continue forward on Northdown Lane, a surfaced public bridleway. Where it goes right in front of residences continue on a narrower enclosed track leading uphill, soon bearing half left on an obvious track up the hill. At the top of the hill at a T-junction of tracks turn right. And so reach Pewley Down at TQ0075 4897. Continue on past the concrete marker point and in about 150m, just before a hedgerow, bear right on a track leading downhill. Enter a wooded area and later at a T-junction turn left. Exit Pewley Down at a junction of tracks at TQ0178 4856. Cross over the broad track and go forward on the track opposite into a wooded area. The path soon divides into bridleway and footpath. At a cross track *(North Downs Way)* at TQ0198 4840 turn left uphill and soon exit the path at a lane *(Halfpenny Lane)*, here turn left.

In 25m at *"Southernway Cottage"* turn right on a track. Continue on the sandy track ahead. Maintain the track up the hill ignoring others eventually reaching St Martha's church on St Martha's Hill.

Section 7
St Martha's Hill to Ranmore 13.5kms 8½ miles 3¼ hrs

Continue through the churchyard of St Martha's and exit on the east side through a gate. Continue on the broad track downhill alongside a low fence on the right. At an inverse Y-junction continue on ahead. In just over another 100m at a Y-junction at TQ0323 4838 turn left following the North Downs Way downhill. Maintain this path ignoring others, which descends to a lane on a bend.

Turn left by a gate before the lane and immediately turn right on a track parallel to the lane. Later descend steps to cross the lane and continue on the track opposite. In 15m take the right fork at a Y-junction. Where the track emerges from the wooded area bear left across cross tracks and emerge to a wide clearing at Albury Down. *(Take the left more upper level path for the best views walking close to the tree line.)* Eventually the path swings left and uphill and emerges at the car park at Newlands Corner at TQ0430 4927.

With your back to the refreshment building in Newlands Corner car park walk to the left towards the road *(A25)*. Before the road bear right on a track quickly joining the North Downs Way. Continue on the track for a few more metres alongside the road to a point where the path meets the road *(A25)*.

Cross over road and continue on the track opposite. Maintain this track ignoring others. At a broad cross track continue on ahead. Maintain the broad track ahead ignoring others. Walk across a car park *(West Hanger)* and meet a road *(Staple Lane)*.

Cross over the road and continue on the track opposite. Later at a road turn right and in 30m turn left and cross over the road and continue on the track opposite. The path joins another broad track coming in from the right at an inverse Y-junction; continue on ahead in the same direction. At an inverse Y-junction continue on ahead and at the gates to Hollister cottage follow the broad track round to the left and past buildings. Walk on past stables and a wide gate. Carry on ahead ignoring other tracks. At a broad junction of tracks by a concrete water tank on the right at TQ0770 4890 continue on ahead.

After 1.3kms *(¾ mile)* reach a junction of five tracks and another concrete water tank at Gravelhill Gate at TQ0891 4933. Continue on in the same direction and after 600m at a Y-junction bear right. In 50m opposite a notice board *(marked Hackhurst Downs)* turn right through a gap by a gate. After 150m ignore the kissing gate on the right and continue on the main path to reach a small open space at a cross track. Go forward through a kissing gate and into a bushy area. Exit through a kissing gate to a path, here turn right. Follow the path ahead and 15m after a T-junction go through a kissing gate and into Blatchford Down. Go forward across the field and later veer to the left to exit through a kissing gate.

Cross over a cross track and go through a second kissing gate and on across a small open green area and eventually reach a gate. Go through the gate and go forward over an offset cross track by a WWII pillbox and on ahead. In 250m at a dip in the path, turn right down a short downhill path to reach a road. Here turn right and in 20m turn left to continue along the North Downs Way. Follow this path for 500m and go through a kissing gate and on ahead. In a further 500m reach a T-junction by a WWII pillbox. Here turn left through a gate and walk uphill for 150m. At a Y-junction by a notice board *(signed White Downs)* bear right.

After 700m reach a cross track. Continue on ahead for 650m to a second cross track. Carry on ahead and in a further 700m at a diagonal cross track go forward in the same direction through a gate and into Steer's Field. Cross the field slightly right aiming to the right of a tree line and behind residences. Exit the field in the left-hand corner through a gate and in 80m go through a kissing gate. Here go half-right and up to a T-junction of roads *(Ranmore common Rd /Ranmore Rd)* at Ranmore.

St Barnabas church, Ranmore Photo L Ham

Section 8
Ranmore to Box Hill 4.7kms (3 miles) 1¼ hrs

Cross over the road and go down the lane opposite *(signed Parish Church)*. Pass by the church of St Barnabas, Ranmore *(built in 1859 by George Cubitt MP, first Baron Ashcombe 1892)* and after 500m where the lane goes sharp left go forward along a concrete lane. In 50m turn right and in a further 150m at a junction of tracks turn left. After 200m go through a metal gate and enter Denbies Wine Estate. Carry on ahead and go through a second metal gate. Continue on this track for about 1km to where it turns sharp right downhill. Here continue forward and in 40m at a cross track keep to the main track downhill bearing right. The track descends round the Estate. Go through a gate by a residence and go forward underneath a railway arch and down to a road *(A24)*.

For the Stepping Stones ph, Westhumble turn left along the A24 for 400m and turn left into Westhumble St, the Stepping Stones is on the left.

Cross over the road *(if the road is too busy then detour to a subway, turn left and walk for 400m to go underneath a subway, returning on the other side of the road)* and turn left and in 40m turn right into a small car park. Walk through the car park and exit in the right-hand corner onto a broad track. Carry on ahead to reach the stepping stones over the River Mole. Cross the stepping stones over the River Mole *(If the River Mole is in flood turn left and then cross over the footbridge, turn right and regain the path on the other side of the stepping stones)* and proceed along the path ahead. The path then goes uphill steeply using a series of steps. At the top at a T-junction of paths turn right and in about 200m arrive at the observation and trig point on Box Hill at TQ1797 5118.

Which way now guys?

The Surrey Hills

Local History Notes

1. Abinger Common

1a. Described as the oldest village in England since it was probably inhabited as long ago as 5000BC by Mesolithic hunter gatherers.

1b. The Normans found Abinger sufficiently important that they built a Motte here. This small castle mound was built around 1100AD and is the earliest known example in Britain with water defences. The Manor house is in Sutton Lane.

1c. Goddard's is a Lutyens house built in 1898-9 by Frederick Mirrelees of "Pasturewood" as a holiday house for "ladies of small means" living in London. It was later sold as a private residence. It is situated opposite the village well.

1d. St James's well on the village green was erected by William John Evelyn in 1893 for the use of the parishioners.

1e. In August 1944 a flying bomb largely destroyed St James's church. Outside the church lych-gate stand the village stocks.

2. Abinger Hammer

2a. Abinger Hammer is situated at the confluence of the Tillingbourne and the Fulvens Brook. The Tillingbourne was dammed to create the hammer ponds to enable iron masters to carry out their craft. Though the ponds are used by watercress growers the water used is said not Tillingbourne water. Local tradition is that guns and munitions made here were used at sea against the Spanish Armada.

2b. The clock that protrudes over the road was given in memory of Lord Farrer of Abinger Hall. The smith on the clock is a clock-jack. He is known locally as "Jack" - Jack the Hammer, a recent idea probably thought up by visitors. The inscription on the clock reads; *"By me you know how fast to go"*, and on the other side it reads; *"for you at home I part the day work and play twixt sleep and meals"*. Abinger Hall no longer exists it was also the location where Charles Darwin studied the earth worm as well as at Leith Hill Place, home of his close relatives – the Vaughan Williams family.

2c. E.M. Forster (1879-1970) lived in a house called *West Hackhurst* at Abinger Hammer. He had often stayed with his aunt in the house that he came to live in himself from 1925 until 1945. The house was originally designed by Forster's father. It was left to Forster by his Aunt Laura. Forster lived here with his mother Lily who died in 1925. Both Lily and Laura are buried in the churchyard of St Mary's at Holmbury St Mary. The house is located up Hackhurst Lane and to the left and beyond a residence called *High Hackhurst* by a footpath which goes towards Piney Copse, sometimes referred to as Forster's Wood. Forster entitled his 1936 collection of essays "Abinger Harvest".

2d. George Meredith who wrote *"Diana of the Crossways"* is said to have been set at Crossways Farm, Abinger Hammer although the site bears no resemblance to the description in the book.

The Surrey Hills

3. Abinger Observatory (site of) Sheephouse Lane at TQ1290 4400
On this eight acre site was situated a Magnetic Observatory in 1924. It had been moved from Greenwich as an alternative location where interference from railways and the electrification of the tramways were minimized. When the electrification of local railway lines in 1937 took place a proposed move to Devon was later delayed due to WWII. Just before the outbreak of WWII, and because of the importance of time signals and the vulnerability to air attack at Greenwich, the Time Department was also re-located here. It was from this site during WWII that the "radio pips" for news broadcasts, transmitted from Rugby, was originated. The site remained active until finally re-located to Hartland Point, Devon in January 1957. There were originally four boundary stones but only two remain together with an azimuth stone used for calibrating their instruments, these can be seen at the northern end of the site at TQ1276 4425. The two boundary stones being about 100m apart.

4. Abinger roughs
  Samuel Wilberforce memorial
Samuel Wilberforce was a highly successful Victorian clergyman and one of the greatest public speakers of the day. Samuel Wilberforce is best remembered for his legendary encounter with Thomas Huxley. The two men publicly argued the case for and against Darwin's controversial theory of evolution by natural selection.

(The inscription reads: This monument marks the spot where Samuel Wilberforce third son of abolitionist William Wilberforce and himself Bishop of Winchester from 1869 to1873 was killed on the 19th July 1873 after a fall from his horse whilst riding with Lord Granville.)

(Huxley commented that Wilberforce's brains had at last come into contact with reality and the result had been fatal.)

Wilberforce was on his way from Leatherhead to dine with the Leveson Gowers and the Gladstones at Holmbury House at the time of the accident.

5. Albury
5a. A mill and a church were recorded at Albury in the Domesday Book. Once known as Weston Street it migrated sporadically down the Tillingbourne valley from the great house of Albury Park from around 1780 onwards. Up to the 1960's the village had a Post Office, Butcher, Baker, Haberdasher, Chemist, Garage, Dairy, Men's Tailor, Photographer, Grocer and Undertaker.

5b. William Oughtred, who invented the use of (x) as the multiplication sign was rector from 1610-1660, he was also tutor to Christopher Wren. He is buried in the Old Saxon church in Albury Park.

5c. Dr Maurice Burton the well-known naturalist and author lived at Weston House until his death in 1992 aged 94.

5d. A Tudor pigeon house stands in Weston Yard. It housed over 600 pigeons which were kept for their meat in winter and also for their droppings which were used as fertilizer and in the manufacture of gunpowder at Chilworth.

5e. Albury Mill dates back to 1255. In 1830 a man called Warner was found guilty of burning it down, he was the last man in England to hang for arson. Milling was moved to Postford Lower Mill in 1910 at which time Albury Park was illuminated by electricity produced by turbines in Albury Mill.

5f. Opposite the mill at Albury House was once owned by the artist Anthony Devis known locally as the "Man Mushroom" because he was the first person to be seen locally underneath an umbrella. Another owner of the house was Martin Tupper (1810-1889) the Victorian poet and writer noted for *"Proverbial Philosophy"* and *"Stephan Langton"*. Martin Tupper is buried in St Peter and St Paul churchyard.

5g. Albury Hall was once a school and a library. Next to Albury Hall is the old Schoolmaster's s House.

5h. *"Not the Old Pharmacy"*, in the main street, now a private residence, was once a haberdashers then a doctor's surgery then a chemist. When it was sold in 1957, the new owners were not allowed to call their house *"The Old Pharmacy"*, so it was named *"Not the Old Pharmacy"*.

5i. The Albury cricket ground is famous for the wartime gathering of Canadian troops who were addressed by Gen *(later Field Marshall)* Montgomery just before the D-Day landings. Monty stood on his jeep and briefed the troops; a stone cairn with an inscription marks the spot.

6. Albury Park

6a. Records of Albury Park date back to the mid 11th century when the manor was held by Azor from Edward the Confessor.

6b. The house in Albury Park is a large Queen Anne country mansion, the interior altered by Sir John Soane in 1802, the exterior re-built in Gothic style in 1847 when more than 40 ornate brick chimneys were added. The 14 acres of park and gardens were laid out in 1667 by John Evelyn.

6c. A Catholic Apostolic church and Chapter House was built by Henry Drummond (1786-1860), twice an MP and a wealthy banker, for the Irvingite Sect in the late 1830's. The church now remains closed awaiting the Second Coming.

6d. Martin Tupper lived at Albury Park from 1850-60.

6e. William Cobbett MP rode across Albury Park on his *Rural Rides*.

7. The Old Saxon church, Albury Park

7a. The maintenance of the fabric of the Old Saxon Church had long been a concern for the parish. In 1820 its seventeenth century spire had become so unsafe that it had to be replaced by the present cupola. A decade later further repairs and refurbishment were needed, and it had become clear that its graveyard could not accommodate the needs of the parish much longer. These problems of the Old Church became a factor in Henry Drummond's scheme for the parish and the Catholic Apostolic Church. By the late 1830's Drummond had conceived a plan which would provide the Apostolic Church with a new and significant dedicated church building; it would give Albury parish a new

The Surrey Hills

Parish Church, and would, incidentally, provide a mortuary chapel in the Old Saxon Church for his family. His plan would mark the final step in the removal of Albury village from the park.

7b. William Oughtred, mathematician and tutor to Christopher Wren, the rector of Albury 1610-1660, is buried here.

8. Betchworth

8a. There was once a castle here on the knoll above the river remains of it are still visible.

8b. There are memorials in St Michael's to, Sir Benjamin Brodie surgeon to Queen Victoria. To Thomas Morsted surgeon to Henry V was at Agincourt, and also to Dyce Duckworth (1840-1928).

8c. There are original 16th century cottages in the village on the lane that leads to Leigh.

8d. Betchworth house built in 1634 was the Manor House.

9. Blackheath

Blackheath is a small hamlet on the edge of Blackheath forest.

10. Box Hill

10a. Box Hill was a gift by Leopold Salomons of 230 acres of land to the National Trust. It is commemorated by the viewing platform looking south over the Weald. Box Hill was the scene of the picnic in Jane Austen's *Emma*. During the 1930's it was the location chosen by many Londoner's for a day in the country. They arrived by train at Westhumble station then called Box Hill. The round tower on Box Hill, known as Broadwood's folly and commemorates *"Waterloo"*, was built by Thomas Broadwood, a piano maker who bought the Juniper Hall in 1814.

Box Hill fort was built in 1888 due to the unstable political situation in Europe and potential threat of invasion; these forts were storehouses and mobilisation centres and extended for 73 miles from Guildford to Halstead *(Kent)*. The idea of forts was abandoned in 1908 in preference for naval protection. The caretaker's cottage at the fort is now a National Trust shop.

Box trees seem to have grown abundantly at Box Hill since at least the sixteenth century. The wood, so hard that it can be carved precisely, is used to make the blocks for wood engravings: the nineteenth-century wood-engraver Thomas Bewick claimed that one of his blocks was still sound after 900,000 printings. Chessmen, carpenters' rules, shuttles for the silk industry, parts of musical instruments and decorative inlay for fine furniture are all made from the box tree. During the First World War boxwood was cut for use in munitions.

Over a dozen species of orchid have been recorded and at least 400 species of other flowering plants: as many as 30 or 40 different plants per square metre may be found in the botanically most important areas such as Juniper Top. But the show-stoppers are the butterflies: Box Hill provides a habitat for a staggering 40 of the 58 British species,

The Surrey Hills

10b. Major Peter Labelliere
On the path leading to the top of Box Hill, a standing stone commemorates the eccentric life of Major Peter Labelliere, an officer of Marines, who for many years was a resident of Dorking. An early 19th-century book called "Promenade round Dorking" relates that 'in early life he fell in love with a lady, who, although he was remarkably handsome in person, eventually rejected his addresses - a circumstance which could not fail to inflict a deep wound on his delicate mind'. Having accurately prophesied the date of his death in 1800, Major Labelliere left two express wishes in his will: that the youngest son and daughter of his landlady should dance on his coffin, and that he should be buried upside down on Box Hill. 'As the world is turned topsy-turvy,' he reasoned quite correctly, it might be argued, he would be the right way up in the end!

10c. River Mole stepping stones
A series of stepping stones in shallow water affords a crossing point at the foot of Box Hill. There is a nearby footbridge in the event of the River Mole being in flood. *(The original footbridge was built in 1932 and replaced in 1946 by Rambler's in memory of those Rambler's who did not return from WWII.)* In 1946, at the expense of the Home Secretary James Chuter-Ede, Clement Atlee declared open the renewed stones.

10d. Flint cottage, Zig Zag Rd, Box Hill
The writer George Meredith (1828-1909) lived at Flint Cottage. In 1864 when he married his second wife Marie Vulliamy he moved from Esher to Flint Cottage. He wrote in a study he had built at the top of the garden. When Marie died in 1889 he remained at Flint Cottage until his own death. He is buried in Dorking cemetery. He wrote *"Dianna of the Crossways"* said to have been set at Crossways Farm, Abinger Hammer. He boarded at Weybridge after his marriage to Thomas Peacock's daughter and later settled at Lower Halliford. She deserted him in 1858, after which he moved to a house near Esher. Among the visitors to Flint Cottage were Leslie Stevenson, Rudyard Kipling, JM Barrie, Henry James and Wilfred Blunt. Leslie Stevenson's Society of Sunday Tramps met to climb Box Hill and Leith Hill with Meredith.

10e. Stane Street
Stane Street is a 56¼ mile long Roman road from London to Chichester coming down through Kennington, Clapham, Balham Merton, Ewell, Epsom, Mickleham and passes through Dorking where there was a Posting station. It crossed the River Mole on a ford at present day Burford Bridge and continues on across Mickleham Downs.

10f. White Hill
An area of Gallops used for leisure purposes by the local wealthy landowners of the area. It now affords pleasant walking and fine views.

10g. Juniper top
This hill offers good distant views to the north and overlooks Juniper Hall.

10h. Juniper Hall
Originally the Royal Oak coaching inn, Juniper Hall was enlarged and remodeled by Sir Cecil Bishop in the 1750s, with a classical portico, tall arched windows and delicate plasterwork inside. Its chief glory was the so-called

sculptured drawing-room, decorated by a gifted amateur artist in the style of Robert Adam. Juniper Hall gave shelter in 1792 to a group of progressive French aristocrats who had fled to England to escape the worst excesses of the French Revolution. It was here also that Fanny Burney, the novelist, first met Alexandre d' Arbley to whom she was subsequently married at Mickleham church. Juniper Hall is now a field study centre.

11. Broadmoor

11a. Broadmoor is a tiny hamlet at the terminal point of a single track lane leading off Sheephouse Lane off the A25 at Wotton.

11b. In the area of Broadmoor Tower *(18th century)*, which sits on a promontory between two valleys, Oswald Moseley's blackshirts *(perhaps unofficially)*, held meetings in secrecy during the 1930's. The remains of the tower have been fenced off due to damage.

11c. The Tillingbourne Waterfall is in the grounds of Lonesome Lodge and which was constructed about 1740.

12. Brockham

12a. W G Grace once played cricket here on the green. Brockham's claim to fame is that it holds the biggest Guy Fawkes bonfire in Surrey.

12b. Along the North Downs Way there were chalk pits and lime works producing hearthstone and firestone as well as lime for agricultural use. The works were known for the Brockham Continuous Lime Kiln patented there in 1889. Bricks continued to be produced there into the 20th century.

13. Burford Bridge hotel

13a. It was formerly called the Fox and Hounds and later the Hare and Hounds and was the location where John Keats completed his poem *Endymion*. Robert Louis Stevenson wrote part of *The New Arabian Nights* here. Other notables to visit here were Queen Victoria, Jane Austen, Wordsworth and Sheridan

13b. Horatio Nelson sometimes visited this hotel with Emma Hamilton. On the night of the 13th and 14th of September 1805 Nelson stopped for a while at this hotel on his way to Portsmouth prior to the Battle of Trafalgar, this was his final night alive on English soil. (See *The Nelson Way* by Les Ham).

13c. Part of the hotel is a tithe barn dating from 1600. It was originally at Abinger before being dismantled and brought here in 1934, it is now the banqueting hall it features beams from ships of the Spanish Armada.

14. Chantry woods

The Chantries or Chantry Woods got their names from the chantry set up in 1486 by Henry Norbridge. In the middle ages a chantry was an endowment which paid for a priest to pray, or sing for the souls of the dead.

15. Cherkley Court

One of the many houses built by the wealthy emigrants from London who preferred the new idyll of country living.

The Surrey Hills

16. Chilworth

16a. Chilworth was built on the site of an 11th Century monastery recorded in the Domesday Book.

16b. Chilworth Manor was built in the 1650's by Vincent Randall from gunpowder production, but there is evidence of materials dating back much earlier *(a fireplace dated 1609)*.

16c. Halfpenny Lane so called due to toll being levied on the cattle drovers using it as a short cut to Guildford market.

16d. The Percy Arms dates back before the 1880's, the ground floor was sometimes used as a mortuary for casualties from the gunpowder works. It was frequented by Canadian troops during WWII when beer was 4d per pint.

16e. On Blacksmiths Lane there was a WWII pillbox built into the end of a cottage, now a fish farm.

17. Chilworth Gunpowder Mills
A Damnable Invention
William Cobbett visited Chilworth in 1822 and was moved to condemn the effect upon the Tillingbourne valley of one of the most damnable inventions that ever sprang from the minds of man under the influence of the Devil, mainly the making of gunpowder.

The East India Company established the Chilworth gunpowder mills in 1626 to make gunpowder for its own use. The Company operated the mills for 10 years which then passed on to the Evelyn Family *(as in John Evelyn the diarist who lived at Wotton)*. The powder came down the Wey Navigation and the River Thames to Barking Creek. Chilworth's market changed in 1790 when other mills opened. For a brief period it was taken over by a German company in 1885 to develop a nearly smokeless powder. At that time Chilworth Manor became the home of the German manager Capt Otto Bouvier from 1887-1906. Six men were killed in an explosion at the gunpowder works in 1901. Chilworth's gunpowder mills were sought out by a Zeppelin raid during WWI but killed only a swan. A second mill was built at Chilworth during WWI. Mergers in 1926 led to the formation of ICI, Chilworth had closed in 1920.

18. Chinthurst Hill

18a. The tower is a 20th Century folly. The height of the hill is just less than 400ft.

18b. Chinthurst Hill Lodge is an Edwin Lutyens house; the gardens were laid out by Gertrude Jekyll.

19. Coldharbour

19a. The village is 700ft up on a greensand ridge and below Leith Hill.

19b. Nearby is Anstiebury Camp one of the largest hill forts in Surrey covering 11 acres within triple banks and ditches. Oval in shape it dates from the 1st or 2nd Century. In the event of a Napoleonic invasion in the 1800's plans were made to shelter women and children of Dorking at Anstiebury

The Surrey Hills

20. Deepdene
20a. Disraeli wrote much of "Coningsby" at Deepdene.

20b. Deepdene House now replaced by Kuoni House, the gardens were first laid out in the 17th C by Charles Howard later extended by Thomas Hope in the 19th C. Thomas Hope (1769-1831) lived here as did Henry Thomas Hope (1808-1862) – he of the Hope diamond, and paintings by Vermeer. At the turn of the 20th century it was leased to Lily, dowager Duchess of Marlborough and aunt of Winston Churchill, who often visited her there.

21. Denbies
21a. The "House on the Hill" called Denbies has had many owners over the years. Denbies was re-built by Thomas Cubitt, who built Osbourne on the Isle of Wight for Queen Victoria. *(The original house no longer stands)*

21b. Denbies is now a prosperous English vineyard of note and well worth a visit.

22. Dorking
22a. Dorking was a Roman settlement on Stane St. There was probably a posting station in Dorking but no trace remains. Posting stations were 12-15 miles apart and consisted of an embankment some 2.5-4 acres in a rectangle and comprised of an Inn, stables and a few houses.

22b. The place name "Deorc Ingas" has 7th/8th C origins and means the people of the Deorc. Dorking is first mentioned in the Domesday Book in 1086 - Dorchinges.

22c. There was a market here by 1268.

22d. In 1664 it had 185 households in the Hearth Tax Returns.

22e. Daniel Defoe was at a boarding school here 1672-6.

22f. John Wesley preached in Dorking in 1764, 1770, 1772, 1775 and 1790.

22g. Dorking was an important agricultural centre emphasized by its own breed of five clawed Dorking chicken which is the town's emblem.

22h. St Martin's church main body was completed in 1873 and replaces two previous churches. The tower and spire (210ft) were added in 1874 as a memorial to Bishop Wilberforce.

22i. The Congregational church in West St houses the organ from the Brighton Pavilion.

22j. Developments of a new bridge over the Pipp brook in 1786 ensured a daily mail coach into Dorking from London. Pippbrook became the council offices in 1931 and now houses the Dorking Library.

22k. During WWII many bombs and incendiaries fell in and around the Dorking area, 5 fell in one night on 21 July 1944.

22l. The Chuter-Ede house on the London Rd was once the house of Clement Attlee's father and grandfather.

22m. Authors
George Gissing (1794-1871) lived at Clifton Terrace, Cliftonville, Dorking.
Denham Jordan (1835-1920) Dorking.
John Mason (1706-1763) was a minister at Dorking.
Walter Thornbury (1828-1876) Dorking.

22n. The Nower – The name "Nower" first appeared when it was owned by Thomas ate Nore in the 14th century. With its copy of the Greek temple of Venus built in 1844 it was donated to the town in 1931 by Lt Col Barclay of the well-known brewery family.

22o. The Glory Wood was named after a group of Scottish firs which crowns the hill top.

22p. The Battle of Dorking – a piece of entertainment:
In the early 1870's Britain was reasonably prosperous but our naval fleet was scattered and our regular army stretched, with troops in India, Canada and Ireland. Germany annexed Holland and Denmark then threatened Britain. After a feint towards Harwich which resulted in the British fleet being all but destroyed and our Army wrong-footed, the German forces attacked from the South, landing at Worthing. The Volunteers, now our last ditch defense force, were sent by train towards Horsham. They arrived too late and retired to Leith Hill. However German columns advancing to the East and West in a pincer movement caused a further retreat through Coldharbour and Dorking. The force finally attempted to defend the line of the North Downs and the key Dorking Gap.

Determined to hold Box Hill to the east and Ranmore to the west, the Volunteers marched through Dorking *(looting a baker's shop on the way)*. An initial attack was repulsed but, lured into a trap when pursuing retreated German troops down the slope from Denbies, our troops were driven back in confusion. After fighting along the road leading from Dorking to Ranmore our troops retreated through Leatherhead and Epsom to Surbiton, where they attempted to regroup. However the Volunteers were no match for the advancing German forces and they were quickly overwhelmed. In the resulting peace Germany annexed the colonies, Ireland became independent and, with the overseas markets for our manufactured goods gone, Britain was finished.

The Volunteer's account of this Battle of Dorking is not strictly accurate. Indeed, even in its totality, it is not in the least bit accurate for it is an imaginary account by Colonel, later General Sir George Chesney MP. But the story was more than simple entertainment. It drew attention to the state of British defenses in the 1870's which had the effect of reinvigorating the British Navy and resulted in improved defenses around London.

22q. Chart Park
Chart Park, Dorking golf Club now occupies the slope below Deepdene Terrace. The park was once the site of an elegant Gothic Mansion dating back to the 17th century; it was demolished in the early 19th century.

23. Duke of Kent School

The 1880s mansion which dominates the school was built by the Doulton family of *"Royal Doulton"*. The estate became a school known as *'Woolpit'* after the Second World War. The RAF Benevolent Fund merged its school with Woolpit in 1976 to form the Duke of Kent School. Since 1997, the school has been a separate charitable institution, still providing education for the children of RAF service people, including foundationers, but increasingly also serving the needs of families from the immediate area as well as boarders from further afield.

24. Ewhurst

Ewhurst windmill at TQ078 427 is a tarred tower with ogee cap, built in 1845 at 800ft it is now a residence. It ceased working in 1885 and lay derelict for many years before being restored in the early years of the 20th century. The original old mill was said to be a landmark for smugglers who used the sunken lanes of The Hurtwood to take contraband from the coast at Shoreham to their London markets.

25. Farley Green

25a. Shophouse Lane did once have a shop.

25b. There are the remains of a Roman Temple on Farley Heath Rd at TQ0517 4493.

26. Friday Street

26a. Friday Street a hamlet which is part of the Wotton Estate is on a tributary of the Tillingbourne here dammed to create a hammer pond.

26b. The mill pond served a corn mill (late 16th C – 1736) and possibly an earlier gunpowder mill.

26c. Stephen Langton (c1156-1228), King John's Archbishop of Canterbury, Biblical scholar and ecclesiastical politician who helped in the making of the "Magna Carta" was thought to be born here, however historians dispute this, some believe that he was born at Langton, Lincolnshire or Norfolk.

27. Gasson Farm

Around the turn of the century Adah Franks, an artist and suffragette, lived here. In the 1930s it was the home of the Canon of Westminster, the Rev. Percy Dearmer. Percy Dearmer was a Christian socialist and author of '*A Parson's Handbook*' and editor of '*The English Hymnal*'.

28. Guildford

"The prettiest and taken altogether the most agreeable and happy looking town that I saw in my life" so said William Cobbett. Guildford sits on the river Wey. The area was likely settled in the early 500's in what was probably called Gyldforda – the Golden Ford, thought to be suggested by the yellow flowers by the riverside. In AD900 Guildford was mentioned in the will of Alfred the Great. By the end of the 10th century it had its own mint. The Castle dates from after the Norman Conquest, the existing keep dates from the 12th century. Henry III lived here as a child. George Abbot, a local man, became Archbishop of Canterbury, he founded the Hospital of the Blessed Trinity

(Almshouses) in 1619. The Tudor grammar school was founded in 1509. Archbishop Abbott, Speaker Onslow and artist John Russell were pupils at the Royal Grammar School. The clock tower projects over the street from a Tudor building re-fronted with a balcony in 1683. Tunsgate was created as a corn market. The Angel Hotel is a 17th century coaching inn. The River Wey was canalized to Guildford in 1653. Lewis Carroll lived and died at The Chestnuts, Castle Hill and is buried at St Michaels. The Guildford to Reigate railway was built in 1849.

29. Gomshall

29a. Pronounced Gumshall. Gomshall mill is early 17th Century.

29b. There is a 16th Century packhorse bridge over the Tillingbourne here.

29c. The King John House, the main parts date from the early 17th century but parts could date from the 16th century. Located at A25/Queen St junction it was formerly Tannery House or Old Tannery House and later Ivy House. An old tradition that the house was built shortly after the Great Plague in 1665 from profits from hides collected free in London is unsupported.

30. Holmbury St Mary

30a. Before 1879, the same year as was built St Mary's church, Holmbury St Mary was known as Felday.

30b. It has been written that E M Forster's novel *"Room with a View"* are precise descriptions of the village.

30c. Holmdale built by G.E.Street was visited by Gladstone and the Cabinet in 1880. G.E. Street was the designer of the London Law Courts and Paddington station in London.

30d. In 1879-80 Edwin Waterhouse (1841-1917) founder of the accountancy firm Price Waterhouse, built a country mansion here called Feldemore, which is now Belmont School.

30e. At the junction of Pitland Street/Horsham Rd there is a cottage on the corner where Victor E Yarsley, Plastics Pioneer and Consultant lived.

31. Holmbury Hill fort

31a. Iron Age Celts settled on Holmbury Hill building a fort which covered eight acres. At 857ft and dating from 150BC-50AD there is evidence to suggest that the fort was hastily abandoned. Artefacts from this site can be seen at Guildford Museum.

31b. Overlooking the Weald view there is a memorial seat in memory of Reginald and Jocelyn Bray who gave the Hurtwood to the public "for air and exercise".

32. Leith Hill

32a. The highest place in southern England rising to 965 feet. From the top of the hill there are magnificent views of the Weald and the South Downs in the distance.

The Surrey Hills

32b. The composer Ralph Vaughan Williams (1872-1958) lived on Leith Hill, at Leith Hill Place (see note 33), and with E M Forster (1879-1970) and others created the annual *(April)* Leith Hill Festival in Dorking.

32c. In 1942 an ammunition dump between Friday Street and Leylands caught fire and scattered ammunition over Leith Hill, it was sealed off until 1955 until the army cleared it all away. They found 250 mines and bombs.

33. Leith Hill Place

This was Ralph Vaughan Williams' (1872-1958) home from the age of three until he left the Royal College of Music although he was a regular visitor thereafter. He inherited the property in 1944 but left the house and the surrounding area to the National Trust. The house had been built in c1600 and bought by RVW's maternal grandfather, Josiah Wedgwood. *(Vaughan Williams was related through his mother to the Darwin and the Wedgwood families. He lived also briefly at The Old Barn, Holmbury St Mary, Glorydene, St Pauls Rd and The White Gates off Westcott Rd.)* Charles Darwin studied the earth worm here. *(See also Abinger Hall note 2b.)*

34. Leith Hill Tower

At Leith Hill, stands a tower adding a further height in total with Leith Hill to top 1000ft. It was built by Richard Hill, by permission from Mr Evelyn of Wotton, as a Prospect Tower in 1765. It is possible to ascend to the top of the tower by a spiral internal stairway. Richard Hill was buried underneath the tower. There is a refreshment kiosk at its base *(restricted opening days in the summer months)*.

35. Mickleham

35a. A churchyard plate commemorates Douglas Gilmour, a flyer who was the first person to be killed in flight in Richmond Park in 1912. He set off from Brooklands in a new monoplane intending to fly to London along the River Thames, when, over Richmond Park one of the wings fell off and he plunged 300 feet to the ground.

35b. St Michael's church has a Norman foundation. Fanny Burney was married there, as was George Meredith.

35c. In 1755 the turnpike road system was extended from Leatherhead to Mickleham, and thence, over a newly constructed bridge at Burford to Giles Green, 200 yards north of Pixham Lane. Here was the Dorking toll gate eight miles from Epsom.

35d. Authors
James Mill wrote on the history of India, Government and mental philosophy.
John Stuart Mill (1806-73) Philosopher and political economist sometimes lived here with his father James Mill (1773-1849).
Joseph Kay (1821-1878) lived at Fredley, Mickleham.
Anne Manning (1807-1879) is buried in Mickleham churchyard.
Winthrop Mackworth Praed (1806-1873) lived at Birch Grove, Mickleham.
Richard Sharp (Conversationalist Sharp) (1759-1835) lived at Fredley Farm, Mickleham.
Samuel Weller Singer (1783-1858) Mickleham.

Marie Carmichael Stopes (1880-1958) lived at Norbury Park, Mickleham. She was married to AV Roe founder of the aircraft firm.

35e. William Whiteley founder of the department store lived at Bencombe, London Rd, Mickleham. Richard Bedford Bennet, Canadian Prime Minister 1932 lived at Juniper Hill, Mickleham.

35f. At Fredley cottage lived "Conversation Sharp" who was sometimes visited by William Wordsworth.

36. Mickleham Downs
36a. Signs of activity date back over 3000 years, during later Roman times the hill tops were used for sheep and the fields in the valleys were given over to crops.

36b. W H Cullen, the grocer lived at Mickleham Downs.

37. Milton Court
37a. The present house was erected in the late 16th century, being re-built in 1611 by Richard Evelyn. It was transformed in the late 19th century for the owner Lachlan Mackintosh Rate by William Burgess. During WWII it was used as offices and quarters when Henleys staff relocated from London.

37b. Author Jeremiah Markland (1693-1763) lived at Milton Court.

38. Newland's Corner
38a. Newland's corner is 567ft (173m) high and has magnificent views of the Greensand hills from the North Downs.

38b. Agatha Christie staged her disappearing act here. Her car was found abandoned with her driving licence and shoes, 30 yards from the road on a cart track. The Surrey Advertiser of the 11 Dec 1926 reported that people turned out in large numbers to search the area. Silent Pool was dragged. She re-appeared 13 days later at the Hydro Hotel, Harrogate but never explained.

39. Norbury Park
39a. Norbury Park House built in the 18th C by William Lock to take advantage of the view over the River Mole to the surrounding hills.

39b. Dr Marie Charlotte Carmichael Stopes (1880-1958) botanist and advocate of birth control lived at Norbury Park. Marie Stopes was married to A V Roe founder of the aircraft firm.

39c. The first flying bomb in WWII fell in Norbury Park on 18th June 1944.

40. Peaslake
40a. At Peaslake once lived 14 ladies of advanced views, among them a Mrs Brackenbury and her two daughters, all of whom were convicted of breaking shop windows in London for the purpose of advertising themselves and their cause. Mrs Brackenbury was 79 years old when she broke windows and went to prison for the suffragette cause. Born in 1832 in Quebec, Hilda Eliza Campbell married Lt Brackenbury and came to live in England. There were no roads in

Peaslake until 1900, and no buses until 1925. Beyond Gomshall people were considered "outsiders".

40b. Here are special burial grounds for the "Quakers" on the land of Thomas Seaman, Lawbrook Lane. Between 1671 and 1716 45 Quaker burials took place. When after 4 deaths the local Quakers declined. The place was known locally as *"Burying Place"*. Lord Ashcome purchased *"Burying Place"*, house, land and orchard. The house was restored and called *"Quakers Garth"*. Later in the 1930's it was re-named to *"Quakers Orchard"*. It was the country home of Sir Adrian Boult.

40c. Frederick William, Baron Pethick-Lawrence of Peaslake (1871-1961) and Emmeline Pethick-Lawrence (1867-1954) who lived at Fourways, Red Lane, Peaslake were both campaigners for women's suffragette. Mr Pethick-Lawrence was later raised to the peerage after his work on Indian Independence. Mahatma Gandhi visited him here in 1933.

40d. Buried in Peaslake cemetery are:
Marion Wallace Dunlop (1864-1942), artist and suffragette, Britain's first hunger striker (5-9 July 1909).
Philibert Merlotte (1880-1961) astronomer and one of the Royal Observatory staff who moved to Abinger during WWII.
Charles Peters (1855-1907) first editor of Girls' Own Paper.
Dorothy Frances Buxton part founder of the Save the Children Fund.

41. Pitch Hill

41a. Pitch Hill is 857ft (257m) high and has superb views of the Weald.

41b. Summerfold House at TQ077 425 was built around 1911 for a Mr Clark. In the 1920s it was owned by the 5th Duke of Sutherland but was not his main residence. His other properties included Sutton Place near Guildford and Dunrobin Castle in Scotland. Summerfold was used mainly for entertaining. He was part of the Duke of Windsor's 'set' and Edward and Wallis Simpson were often his guests. During the Second World War it was occupied by Canadian officers stationed in the area and also used as a 'listening post'. After the war it was left empty and became derelict until its restoration in the 1980s.

41c. The Four Winds was the home of the Rev. Stopford Brooke who was well known in artistic and literary circles. He was friends with Ruskin and Morris, and published many books on literature and poetry. He was already 79 when he built The Four Winds and at first used as it a country retreat. In 1914 he decided to make it his permanent home and spent the last few years of his life there. When he died in 1916 his ashes were scattered in the garden close to his favourite seat.

42. Polesden Lacey

42a. King George VI and Elizabeth spent part of their honeymoon at Polesden Lacey in April 1923.

42b. Richard Brinsley Sheridan (1751-1816) dramatist and MP lived here but in an earlier house.

43. Ranmore
St Barnabas church, Ranmore Common designed by George Gilbert Scott and built by Cubitt has a 150ft spire and from its position can be seen for many miles. Inside is a memorial to 3 of Cubitt's sons killed in WWI.

44. Raynards Hill
Lord Justice James is commemorated here with a seat facing a view over the weald and towards the South Downs.

45. Rookery
In 1759, David Malthus, father of Thomas Malthus, the economist, bought the Rookery estate. Two water mills once stood on the stream. It was the birthplace in 1766 of Robert Malthus.

46. River Mole
Some claim that it takes its name from the animal since, on occasions it flows underground between Dorking and Leatherhead. Others say that the Latin Mola for Mill is the more likely since there were many watermills along its banks.

47. Shalford
47a. Shalford Mill is a 17th century timber frame construction, it was given to the National Trust in 1932 by Major Arthur Goodwin-Austen *(one of the Goodwin-Austen's explored and surveyed the North West Himalayas)*.

47b. Shalford is where the Tillingbourne joins the River Wey.

47c. John Bunyan (1628-1688) is reputed to have lived here for a time. Shalford fair may have suggested Vanity Fair which was held in the meadows to the north. The swampy marshes of Shalford are thought to be Bunyan's Slough of Despond and that the Surrey Hills were the Delectable Mountains.

47d. There is a WWII defensive position outside the *The Seahorse Inn* public house.

47e. Before moving to Albury, William Oughtred well-known as the *"Prince of Mathematicians"* had a European wide reputation, he invented the slide rule, was the Vicar of Shalford 1605-1610. He then became Rector in Albury 1610-1660. He died on 30 September 1669 and is buried in the Old Saxon church in Albury Park.

47f. William Holland of Shalford sailed with Captain Cook, he lived at Debnershe in The Street. He was with Cook's party in Hawaii at the time of Cook's death.

47g. Another Shalford sailor was Thomas Fitzherbert Bartholomew of 34 The Street who at the age of 15 was a midshipman learning the skills of the sea; navigation, gunnery, management of sail and rigging. He was on board the *Swiftsure*, a 74 gun ship of the line, at the Battle of Trafalgar *(See The Nelson Way by Les Ham)*. After the battle the *Swiftsure* took in tow the French ship *Redoubtable*, a sniper from this ship had earlier killed Admiral Lord Nelson. Later the unsteady *Redoubtable* had to be cut a drift. Later Bartholomew fell to his death at midnight from the main mast.

The Surrey Hills

47h. In Shalford churchyard is buried Col Frederick George Shewell who commanded the 8th Hussars during the Crimean War 1854-56.

47i. During the Cold War in the 1950's and 1960's Shalford had a bunker to store emergency food supplies from which rationed supplies would have been issued in the event of a nuclear attack.

48. East Shalford
Just by the Tillingbourne in East Shalford there is a house called *"Merlins"*, which was once a hall house and dates from the 15th century.

49. Shere
49a. Shere is the ancestral home of the Bray family and was given to the Bray family by Henry VII in the 15th century.

49b. There is a brass in St James' church to Lord Audley whose son James was beheaded at the Tower of London for being a leader of the Cornish Rebellion in 1497. James had led his men through Shere on their way to Blackheath in Kent.

49c. The Anchoress of Shere – St James' 1329 – Christine daughter of William the village carpenter was enclosed in building attached to the church. Permission was granted by the Bishop of Winchester and local priests and villagers. She escaped after 3 years but allowed herself to be re-captured and re-enclosed. The slot and the quatrefoil openings still remain in the chancel wall. There is a plaque outside the church on its the north side.

49d. In Shere, lavender, chamomile and mint were grown at The Flower Farm. Herbs were distilled at High House, Shere from 1925-39 beyond the church and to the left. A pre-war advert states that Colebrooks made lavender and violet perfume with a brand name "ESSIRA" which is the Domesday name for Shere.

49e. Sir Edwin Landseer Lutyens (1869-1944), builder of the Cenotaph in London, built the gate lodge to the manor house for Sir Reginald Marc Bray, some cottages nearby and designed the lych-gate to St James' church. He also built the village barbers shop now tea rooms.

49f. J.M.Barrie (1860-1937) lived for a while in 1891 at Anchor Cottage, Upper St is where he wrote *"The Professor's Love Story"*.

49g. Shere had a Barn Theatre in the 1930's where the Otherwise Players performed; one of their players who made his first appearance on stage in 1938 was Peter Ustinov. Another of their players was Herbert Lom. The Barn Theatre was situated at High House Farm behind St James' church.

49h. The drinking fountain was built in 1886 by two local sisters called Spotteswood who wished to provide alternative beverages to the White Horse. It is 280ft deep and flowed until 1970 when the water table was lowered by Thames Water.

49i. Dating back to the 1500's The White Horse started life as a farmhouse named *"Cripps"* standing within two acres of ground known as *"Marysse"*.

Constructed out of ships' timbers, the building is believed to have become an Inn, with its own brew house, in the 17th Century. Local legend linking The White Horse to smuggling appears well-founded after the discovery in 1955 of a hidden cellar containing casks of brandy dating back to 1720.

49j. Shere adopted a ship *(HMS Stornest)* from 1938 until 1941. It was lost in the Atlantic in 1942.

49k. Ft Lt John Vere Hopgood, a dambuster, who flew with Guy Gibson, was killed on the Mohne Dam raid during WWII, lived in Shere. He is commemorated in St James' church, Shere.

49l. Orchard cottage was the HQ of the ARP in WWII.

49m. Authors
George Grote (1794-1871) lived at The Ridgeway, Shere.
Charles Edward Montague (1867-1928) lived at The Ridgeway, Shere.

49n. There was a Lime kiln at London Rd, Shere at TQ074 486. An elongated circular kiln set in a bank on the north side of a sunken lane.

49o. There were charcoal burning kilns on Manor Estate, Shere at TQ079 494. Remains of four "modern" kilns alongside a bridleway at Netley Heath each consisting of an 8ft diameter circular steel base, centre section and conical dome with lid. Cast iron channels set through the base have holes for detachable chimneys.

49p. Above Shere and at the top of Colekitchen Lane at Hackhurst Down near Blind Oak Gate (now private land) stood a shutter telegraph location. This system came into being in 1796 and lasted until 1822 when the Semaphore system was introduced.

50. Silent Pool
More properly Shireborne Pond and location for Martin Tupper's novel *"Stephen Langton"*. Noted for its translucency and also for the legend surrounding it. The whole area used to be part of Windsor Forest and King John, while still a prince would hunt here. One story is that a damsel called Emma who attracted his attention drowned in the pool trying to escape from him and her ghost haunts this place to this day.

51. St Catherine's Hill and chapel ruins
The popular idea was that St Catherine's chapel was a stopping point for pilgrims visiting the shrine of Thomas-A-Beckett at Canterbury.

52. St Martha's Hill
52a. No other church in the country is dedicated to St Martha, the name was first recorded in 1224. A Norman church on the summit of a wooded greensand hill (573ft), it was damaged in the 18th C by an explosion at the nearby gunpowder factory and re-built in the 19th century using carstone.

52b. The idea of Pilgrim's Progress was first thought to originate from John Bunyan visiting this spot.

The Surrey Hills   121

52c. Good Friday dancing took place here until the custom died out around 1900.

52d. Yvonne Arnaud the actress and musician's ashes are scattered here, a commemorative stone is located by the east churchyard gate.

52e. Bernard Freyberg VC *"Man of two nations"* is buried here. The Rt Hon. Bernard Cyril Freyberg, 1st Baron Freyberg, VC, GCMG, KCB, KBE, DSO (March 21, 1889 - July 4, 1963) was a distinguished military leader of New Zealand forces during both World War I and World War II. Freyberg was born in Richmond, Surrey and moved to New Zealand with his parents when he was two years old. He attended Wellington College (New Zealand) from 1897 to 1904. A strong swimmer, he was New Zealand 100 yards champion in 1906 and 1910. He left New Zealand in March 1914, and is known to have been in San Francisco and Mexico, where he may have been involved in the civil war then raging in that country. Upon hearing of the outbreak of World War I in Europe in August 1914, he travelled to England.

In 1914 Freyberg met and persuaded the then First Lord of the Admiralty Winston Churchill to give him a commission into the Hood Battalion of the infant Royal Naval Division. During the initial landing at Battle of Gallipoli Freyberg swam from ship to shore lighting flares to distract the enemy, for this he received his first Distinguished Service Order. He attained command of a brigade (in the 58th Division) in April 1917, reportedly making him the youngest General in the British Army

He received the Victoria Cross during World War I at the Battle of the Somme. On November 13, 1916 at Beaucourt sur Ancre, France, after carrying the initial attack through the enemy's front system of trenches, Lieutenant Colonel Freyberg's battalion was much disorganized, but after rallying and re-forming his own men and some others, he led them on a successful assault of the second objective, during which he was twice wounded, but remained in command and held his ground throughout the day and the following night. When reinforced the next morning he attacked and captured a strongly fortified village, taking 500 prisoners. He was wounded twice more, the second time severely, but he refused to leave the line until he had issued final instructions.

On 14 June 1922 he married Barbara McLaren *(née Jekyll),* a widow with two children, at St Martha on the Hill near Guildford; they would have one son. In the general election of that year he stood unsuccessfully as a Liberal candidate.

Prior to WWII he was classified as unfit for active service by the British Army. In 1937 Freyberg approached the New Zealand government to offer his services upon the outbreak of World War II. He was appointed commander of the New Zealand 2nd Division. In the chaos of the retreat from the Greek mainland campaign of 1941, Freyberg was given command of Allied forces during the Battle of Crete.

After WWII he served as Governor-General of New Zealand from 1946 until 1952. He was raised to the peerage as Baron Freyberg, of Wellington in New

Zealand and of Munstead in the County of Surrey, in 1951. On the March 1, 1953 he was made the deputy constable and lieutenant governor of Windsor Castle, he took up residence in the Norman Gateway the following year. He died at Windsor on July 4, 1963 following the rupture of one of his WWI war wounds, and was buried in the churchyard of St Martha on the Hill, Guildford.

53. Surrey Hills
Weald clay, the wooded Greensand and the Downland chalk were laid down in the Cretaceous period about 100-700BC. The dominant feature of Surrey is the North Downs, a range of chalk hills stretching from east to west. Two rivers cut through the North Downs, the Wey and the Mole.

54. Sutton Abinger
54a. Edward Frances Williams (1903-1970) journalist lived at Griffins, Sutton Abinger

54b. Sir Harold Spencer-Jones, Astronomer Royal set up his office during WWII at Cornerways, Sutton Abinger.

55. Tillingbourne valley
55a. In 1579 George Evelyn was granted by Queen Elizabeth I a monopoly for the manufacture of gunpowder and chose this area because it had water for power and transportation, wood for fuel and yet was sufficiently remote to allow manufacturing to proceed unhindered. Thereafter other industries sprang up, particularly around the numerous mills established on the river: along the 11 mile stretch there are records of a total of 30 mills for corn, cloth, brass, iron, paper and powder. Richard Evelyn introduced wire making and the region produced nails, mousetraps and other products based on the material. There was leather tanning, flax retting, iron manufacture and brewing all underway in the valley. The Tillingbourne valley was the "silicon valley" of its day.

The Tillingbourne is 11 miles in length rising on the dip slope of the Lower Greensand on Leith Hill at the junction of the Hythe Beds and the Atherfield clay and flows into the River Wey at Shalford. Along the length of the Tillingbourne rainfall permeates the greensand to the south and chalk to the north and emerges as springs. Even during the driest summer the flow remains strong; equally in the wettest winter there is little flooding.

55b. The wealthy families of the area were the Malthuses of Milton Court, Hills of Abinger, Barclays, Evelyns of Wotton, Brays of Shere, Morgans and Randalls of Chilworth. There were also the medieval families such as the Westons of Albury.

55c. Some of the mills in the area were:

Mill	Location	Uses
Paddington mill	TQ101471	
Abinger Forge mill	TQ095475	
Abinger mill	TQ110460	Gunpowder converted to copper then "batter" mill (brass and copper plate) In 1670 it was enlarged into three mils (wheat, malt and oats)

Gomshall mill	TQ084478	
Shere lower mill	TQ074479	Domesday site
Shere west mill	TQ068479	Corn mill in 1678
Netley mill	TQ079479	
Albury Park mill	TQ062479	Corn mill destroyed by fire in 1727 and in 1795 it was converted to a paper mill. It closed in the 1820's and later it was used as a laundry.
Postford upper mill	TQ041480	Paper mill – no trace
Postford lower mill	TQ039480	Paper?
Chilworth upper mill		
Chilworth lower mill	TQ025475	Gunpowder and paper
Chilworth middle mill	TQ028475	Gunpowder and paper
Shalford mill	TQ001478	

55d. Tillingbourne Bus Co
The Tillingbourne bus co was started in 1924 serving Dorking, Guildford, Shalford, Little London and Peaslake.

56. Westhumble

56a. Remains of Westhumble 12th century chapel on Chapel Lane was reputedly built as a chapel for pilgrims.

56b. Box Hill and Westhumble railway station built in 1867 for the landowner Thomas Grissell who insisted that it should be built of an ornamental character *(polychrome brick with stone dressing)*.

56c. Stepping Stones public house built around 1870 and originally called the Railway Arms. It was the local ARP wardens post in WWII. It takes its present name from the nearby stepping stones over the River Mole and was re-named in the 1950's.

56d. At Cleveland cottage on Westhumble St there are plaques to Sir James Hopwood Jeans, Physicist, Astronomer and Popularizer of Science (1877-1946) and Lady Susi Jeans, Organist and Scholar (1911-1993) who both lived here. It was previously the Royal School of Church music. *(After research for this book the School has been demolished in 2007 for re-development.)*

56e. John Weller inventor and designer of AC cars lived at Westhumble. J Norton Griffiths, an engineer who was responsible for the building of the Aswan Dam in 1894 lived at Mulberry Cottage, Westhumble.

56f. Authors
Matthew Arnold (1822-1888) lived at Westhumble
Frances Burney (1752-1840) lived at Camilla cottage, Westhumble.
Daniel Defoe (1661?-1731) lived at Burford Corner

57. Westcott

57a. The Bury Hill estate was formed by Edward Walker in the 1730's and was acquired by the Barclay family in 1812. The original estate could date back to 1530.

57b. The village church was built to a George Gilbert Scott design in 1852.

57c. The Hut, Furlong Rd was opened by Princess Marie Louise, grand daughter of Queen Victoria on 15 December 1919 Its original use was to provide a recreational room, library, billiards and smoking room for WWI returnees and is a forerunner of the current village club. It later became HQ of the Red Triangle Club (or YMCA). It was the first Red Triangle Club in England to permit the entry of women over 16.

57d. Leslie Howard, actor (1893-1943) lived at Stowe Marius, Balchins Lane, Westcott. He is probably best remembered for his role as Ashley Wilkes in the Hollywood film *"Gone with the Wind"*. Leslie Howard was killed in June 1943 when the aircraft in which he was flying in was shot down over the Bay of Biscay whilst he was returning from a "lecture" tour in Lisbon. At the time Lisbon was a hotbed of spies. Papers relating to the incident of his death held at the Public Record Office, Kew have been withheld from publication for a further extended period adding further intrigue to this event.

57e. On 7 Jan 1944 a bomb fell in Watson Rd demolishing 4 houses. At the residence of a Mr Wakeford it killed 9 persons. Two of the killed were boys sent down from London to escape the bombing there. There are two wooden seats on the green commemorating the event.

57f. Evidence of WWII still exist as indicated by walls and ditches clearly visible along Milton Heath between Westcott and The Nower, which were originally constructed as an Army assault course.

57g. On 29 July 1948 torch bearer K Vaughan of Herne Hill Harriers carried the Olympic torch through Westcott to Crossways Farm on the A25.

57h. Authors
Thomas Robert Malthus (1766-1834) was born at The Rookery, Westcott.
Abraham Tucker (1705-1774) lived at The Rookery, Westcott.

58. Wey Navigation
The Wey Navigation from the River Thames to Guildford was opened in 1653 and the extension to Godalming opened in 1763. It was linked to the Arun canal in the early 19th century as an alternative route from Portsmouth to London to counter adverse winds on the sea route to the south coast and enemy action during the Napoleonic wars.

59. Wey South Path
This path follows the route of a disused Guildford to Shoreham railway line. It was built in two sections Shoreham to Itchingfield Junction in 1861 and Christ's Church Hospital to Guildford in 1865. The sections were linked by the working Arun Valley line. By 1966 both lines had closed under the Beeching Railway Act.

60. Wonersh
Famous in Elizabethan times for Wonersh Blue, a cloth. Sir Fletcher Norton of Wonersh House was Speaker of the House of Commons 1769-82. The mansion house at Wonersh was demolished in the 1930's.

61. Wotton

61a. Wotton is the ancestral home of the Evelyn family who were a substantial Surrey landowning family whose fortunes were founded in gunpowder manufacture.

61b. John Evelyn (1620-1706) the famous diarist is buried in Wotton church. He lived at Wotton House, Wotton. It is said that John Evelyn received some of his education from the Friar at Wotton church. He was a scholar, connoisseur, bibliophile and horticulturalist, as well as a writer and thinker about relevant issues of the day.

61c. On the night of 24/5 February 1944 a Dornier aircraft was shot down by a Mosquito of No 29 Night Fighter Squadron from Ford in Sussex. Of its crew of four two bailed out and were initially taken by special constable to the Wotton Hatch public house. The other two crew members were killed when the aircraft crashed at Westcott. The Dornier was apparently on its way to King George V docks in London when it was intercepted.

62. Surrey hills WWII

During WWII thousands of high explosives and incendiaries fell in the Surrey. To avoid greater loss of life in London disinformation was released to the Germans that their flying bombs were falling to the north of London. This had the effect of the Germans making fuel and navigational adjustments that had them falling far short of the capital and into less densely populated areas.

63. Surrey hills WWII Pillboxes

Along various paths keep a lookout for wartime "pillboxes". These "pillboxes" formed a defensive chain across England to combat or slow down any invading forces during WW II. They were positioned by roads, lanes, rivers, railway lines or any other vulnerable route. They were mainly manned by the Home Guard - *"Dad's Army"*. Some 20,000 pillboxes were built of which 2,000 survive mainly in rural areas.

History would be an excellent thing if only it were true – Tolstoy

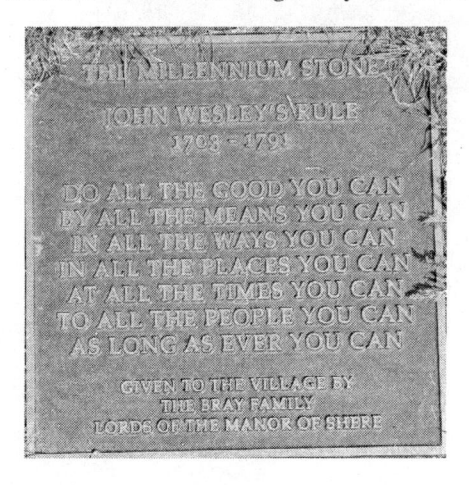

The Millennium Stone plaque in St James' churchyard, Shere Photo L Ham

126   The Surrey Hills

Village Signs

Useful addresses and website

Useful addresses
Rambler's Association, 2nd Floor, Camelford House, 89 Albert Embankment, London SE1 7TW, Tel: 020 7339 8500 Fax: 020 7339 8501
www.ramblers.org.uk Email: ramblers@london.ramblers.org.uk

Ordnance Survey
Tel: 08456 050505 or 023 8079 2000 www.ordnancesurvey.co.uk

National Trust, Tel: 0870 609 5380 www.nationaltrust.org.uk

Countryside Agency, Tel: 020 7340 2900 www.countrside.gov.uk

English Heritage, Tel: 0870 333 1181 www.english-heritage.org.uk

English Nature, Tel: 01733 455100 www.english-nature.org.uk

Streetmap www.streetmap.co.uk

Guide to taxis serving all railway stations www.traintaxi.co.uk

Details of over 3000 taxi firms www.cabnumbers.com

Information on public transport fro countryside visitors www.countrygoer.org

Met Office, Tel 0845 300 03000 www.metoffice.com

Useful websites

www.surreyhills.org

www.nationaltrust.org.uk/northdowns

www.visitsurrey.com

Surrey County Council

www.surrey.gov.uk

www.surrey.gov.uk/passenger_transport

Tourist Information Centres
TIC, Council Offices, South St, Farnham, GU9 7RN Tel: 01252 715109

VIC, Haslemere Educational Museum, 78 High St, Haslemere, GU27 2LA
Tel: 01428 645425

TIC, 14 Tunsgate, Guildford, GU1 3QT. Tel: 01483 444333

VIC, Dorking Halls, Reigate Rd, Dorking, RH4 1SG. Tel: 01306 879327

Travel information
Buses
Traveline
Tel: 0870 608 2608 (0700-2200)
www.traveline.org.uk

Arriva Surrey
Tel: 01483 505693
www.arriva.co.uk

Stagecoach Hants and Surrey
Tel: 0845 121 0180
www.stagecoachbus.com

Surrey County Council Bus and Train guides
No 7 covers areas around Guildford & Cranleigh
No 8 cover areas around Dorking
Both these guides cover the areas of walks in this book

Guildford operates a park and ride facility into the Guildford bus station.

Rail
www.nationalrail.co.uk

South West Trains
www.southwesttrains.co.uk
Tel: 0845 6000 650
Textphone: 0800 692 0792

Museums
Surrey Museums, 130 Goldsworthy Rd, Woking, surrey, GU21 6ND
Tel: 01483 518737
www.surreymuseums.org.uk

Dorking
Dorking & District Museum, The Old Foundry, 62 West St, Dorking, Surrey, RH4 1BS Tel: 01306 876591 www.dorkingmuseum.co.uk
Email: museum13@dorking13.wanadoo.co.uk
Open: Wed & Thu 1400-1700, Sat 1000-1600, groups at other times by appointment.

Shere
Shere Museum, The Malt House, Shere Lane, Shere, Surrey, GU5 9HS
Tel: 01483 203245 Open: Check opening times

Guildford
Guildford Museum, Castle Arch, Guildford, GU1 3SX Tel: 0143 444751
www.guildfordmuseum.co.uk
Email: museum@guildford.gov.uk
Open: All year Mon-Sat 1100-1645

Index

Abinger Bottom, 44, 46
Abinger Common, 31, 33, 44, 45, 46, 55, 56, 104
Abinger Hammer, 82, 85, 86, 104, 108
Abinger Roughs, 31, 32, 33
Albury, 59, 60, 61, 66, 67, 68, 69, 71, 72, 73, 82, 87, 88, 101, 105, 106, 107, 118, 122, 123
Anstiebury, 27, 28, 39, 40, 90, 96, 110
Betchworth, 15, 17, 18, 20, 93, 94, 107
Blackheath, 51, 66, 71, 73, 74, 78, 107, 119
Bookham, 24, 25
Box Hill, 12, 13, 14, 15, 16, 19, 20, 22, 24, 25, 90, 92, 93, 102, 103, 107, 108, 112, 123
Broadford, 78, 79
Broadmoor, 39, 40, 42, 84, 109
Broadstone, 77, 100
Brockham, 15, 17, 18, 90, 92, 93, 94, 109
Brook, 51, 52, 62, 65, 66, 68, 69, 77, 86, 100, 104
Burford Bridge, 12, 14, 15, 18, 19, 90, 108, 109
Chilworth, 71, 78, 80, 82, 88, 105, 110, 122, 123
Chinthurst, 74, 76, 90, 99, 100, 110
Coldharbour, 27, 28, 39, 40, 41, 83, 90, 95, 96, 110, 112
Deepdene, 12, 15, 19, 20, 90, 94, 111, 112
Dorking, 12, 15, 19, 20, 21, 22, 23, 24, 27, 31, 35, 90, 94, 95, 108, 110, 111, 112, 114, 115, 118, 123, 127, 128
East Shalford, 74, 77, 82, 88, 89, 90, 100, 119
Ewhurst, 47, 48, 50, 90, 98, 113
Farley Green, 51, 62, 66, 71, 72, 113
Farley Heath, 51, 53, 68, 72, 99, 113
Friday Street, 35, 36, 38, 39, 43, 113, 115
Gomshall, 55, 58, 59, 62, 63, 82, 86, 87, 90, 114, 116, 120, 122
Holmbury St Mary, 44, 46, 47, 50, 90, 104, 114, 115
Leith Hill, 27, 28, 29, 39, 41, 44, 45, 83, 90, 95, 96, 104, 108, 110, 112, 114, 115, 122
Little London, 51, 62, 65, 66, 71, 123
Mickleham, 12, 13, 15, 19, 108, 109, 115, 116
Milton Heath, 27, 30, 124
Newlands Corner, 59, 60, 66, 67, 70, 90, 101
Peaslake, 51, 52, 54, 62, 64, 65, 90, 116, 117, 123
Pitch Hill, 47, 50, 90, 97, 98, 117
Pitland Street, 44, 90, 97, 114
Portsmouth, 109
Raynards Hill, 47, 49, 50, 90, 118
River Mole, 12, 14, 15, 17, 18, 19, 20, 24, 90, 94, 103, 108, 116, 118, 123
Shalford, 74, 77, 78, 82, 88, 89, 90, 100, 118, 119, 122, 123
Shere, 59, 61, 62, 63, 65, 82, 87, 90, 103, 119, 120, 122, 125, 128
Silent Pool, 66, 69, 70, 116, 120
Somerset Hill, 44, 47, 90, 97
St Martha's, 59, 60, 74, 75, 78, 80, 90, 100, 101, 120
Stane St, 12, 13, 108, 111
Stepping Stones, 12, 15, 19, 23, 24, 25, 26, 90, 103, 123
Stonebridge, 79
Sutton Abinger, 55, 57, 122
The Rookery, 27, 29, 31, 34, 35, 37, 124
Tillingbourne, 27, 31, 33, 34, 35, 38, 39, 40, 57, 59, 63, 66, 67, 77, 80, 82, 83, 84, 85, 86, 87, 88, 89, 90, 100, 104, 105, 109, 110, 113, 114, 118, 119, 122, 123
Waterloo Pond, 74, 75, 76, 82, 88
West Hackhurst, 55, 57, 104
Westcott, 31, 32, 34, 35, 37, 90, 115, 123, 124, 125
Westhumble, 12, 15, 19, 24, 25, 26, 90, 92, 103, 107, 123
Wey Navigation, 78, 79, 82, 89, 110, 124
White Hill, 12, 13, 108
Winterfold Hill, 47, 49, 90, 96, 98
Wonersh, 31, 33, 34, 35, 36, 38, 74, 76, 79, 82, 83, 84, 85, 90, 98, 99, 100, 110, 113, 115, 122, 124, 125
Wotton House, 35, 36, 125

Also by Les Ham

The Orange Way

Following the march of Prince William of Orange from Brixham (Devon) to London in 1688.

350 miles, 176 pages, 44 illustrations, 33 maps
ISBN 1-869922-47-6 Price £9.95

Available from booksellers, or direct from the publishers. Meridian Books, 40 Hadzor Rd, Oldbury, West Midlands, B68 9LA, UK. (Plus £1 p& p)

Or discounted signed copies from the author at:
www.leshambooks.com

The Nelson Way

A long distance walk from Burnham Thorpe in Norfolk (Nelson's birthplace) to HMS Victory, Portsmouth. It links the walker to the unfolding story of Nelson and highlighting the locations that Nelson knew.

424 miles, 210 pages, 43 illustrations, 18 maps
ISBN 1-4120-5475-3 Price £11.49

Available from booksellers or direct from the publishers, Trafford Publishing Ltd, 9 Park End St, 2nd Floor, Oxford, OX1 1HH, UK
Order online www.trafford.com/05-0373

Or discounted signed copies from the author at:
www.leshambooks.com